'It pays dividends'

Direct payments and older people

Heather Clark, Helen Gough and Ann Macfarlane

First published in Great Britain in February 2004 by

The Policy Press
Fourth Floor, Beacon House
Queen's Road
Bristol BS8 1QU
UK

Tel +44 (0)117 331 4054
Fax +44 (0)117 331 4093
E-mail tpp-info@bristol.ac.uk
www.policypress.org.uk

© University College Chichester 2004

Transferred to Digital Print 2008

Published for the Joseph Rowntree Foundation by The Policy Press

ISBN 978 1 86134 580 6

British Library Cataloguing in Publication Data
A catalogue record for this report is available from the British Library.

Library of Congress Cataloging-in-Publication Data
A catalog record for this report has been requested.

Heather Clark is a Senior Lecturer in Sociology and Social Policy in the School of Social Studies, Univeristy College Chichester. **Helen Gough** was a Research Assistant in the School of Social Studies, University College Chichester. **Ann Macfarlane** is a Disability Quality Consultant.

The **Joseph Rowntree Foundation** has supported this project as part of its programme of research and innovative development projects, which it hopes will be of value to policy makers, practitioners and service users. The facts presented and views expressed in this report are, however, those of the authors and not necessarily those of the Foundation.

The statements and opinions contained within this publication are solely those of the authors and not of The University of Bristol or The Policy Press. The University of Bristol and The Policy Press disclaim responsibility for any injury to persons or property resulting from any material published in this publication.

The Policy Press works to counter discrimination on grounds of gender, race, disability, age and sexuality.

Cover design by Qube Design Associates, Bristol
Front cover: photograph supplied by kind permission of www.JohnBirdsall.co.uk
Printed and bound by CPI Group (UK) Ltd, Croydon, CR0 4YY

Contents

Executive summary

Introduction

The 1996 Community Care (Direct Payments) Act authorised local authorities to make cash payments instead of providing services to some people assessed as needing community care services. When the Act was implemented in 1997, its scope was restricted to service users between the ages of 18 and 65. It has, however, since been extended to include people over the age of 65, young people aged 16-17, informal carers aged 16 and over, and people with parental responsibility for a disabled child. Furthermore, while the Act was originally permissive – enabling local authorities to make cash payments in lieu of services, regulations effective from April 2003 imposed a duty upon local authorities to offer direct payments to all those eligible for them.

The government regards direct payments as an important means towards promoting independence, increased choice and control, improved quality of life, and social inclusion. There are now over 1,000 older people receiving direct payments in England, yet little is known about their experiences and there remains scepticism about older people's desire and ability to work with direct payments.

This report is based on research with 41 older people receiving direct payments, 12 care management teams, five senior managers and three direct payments support services. The research was conducted in three English local authority areas; it explores how older people work with direct payments and ways in which local authority care management teams and direct payments support workers can make direct payments work for older people.

Findings and key messages

- The benefits older people derived from direct payments included improved quality of life, greater motivation, and a sense of feeling happier. There was a positive impact on their social, emotional and physical health. They enjoyed life more and felt more relaxed and able to do more for themselves.
- Direct payments enabled some Somali older people to secure culturally relevant services from Personal Assistants (PAs). Accountancy services to deal with bank accounts, and the financial and administrative requirements of direct payments, were identified as essential in overcoming

- language and literacy barriers faced by the older Somali people.
- Older people pointed to the importance of good and timely information about direct payments and suggested the use of national and local radio, and housing, social and community settings to make direct payments better-known among older people.
- Most older people used their direct payments to employ PAs. Those with transferable skills from past career and life experiences often successfully adapted them to help manage PAs. Finding PAs was not easy and there was a call for direct payments support services to compile and maintain registers of potential PAs.
- Some older people used their PAs to pursue social and leisure activities and/or to develop alternatives to institutional respite care. As such activities were rarely included in their care plans, older people had to use their allocated hours creatively and meet the extra costs from their own incomes.
- There were no instances in which health authorities contributed to a direct payment package, and therefore older people were unable to use their payments to purchase health-related services such as chiropody and physiotherapy from professional bodies. Older people found this absurd as these were essential to the maintenance of their health and mobility. They used their PAs to meet some of these needs.
- Meeting audit and administrative demands was the major difficulty faced by the older participants in managing direct payments. They needed ongoing assistance from direct payments support services.

- People crossing the social services administrative boundary between 'adult' and 'older persons'' services when they reached 65 faced new restrictions on their access to leisure and social facilities, and ageist perceptions about older people's lifestyles.
- The exclusion of older people from applying to the Independent Living 93 Fund is discriminatory and neglects the greater financial costs to people experiencing both ageing and impairment.
- No partners and other informal carers had been offered direct payments in their own right. Care management teams knew little of the provisions of the 2000 Carers and Disabled Children Act, while eligibility criteria ruled out the provision of the sort of low-level services, such as domestic assistance, that informal carers needed.
- Direct payments were rarely part of the culture of care management teams. However, there was a commitment to change that.
- To achieve that cultural change, care managers require sufficient knowledge about direct payments, the support and encouragement of their immediate line managers, time to think and work creatively, and a clear understanding of the role of direct payments support services. Joint working with direct payments support services increased care managers' knowledge and confidence.
- Translating a community care assessment into a direct payments package without removing the flexibility that enables the individual to take control is key to the success of direct payments. Care managers, however, faced tensions between, on the one hand, adhering to eligible needs and working within local

budgetary constraints and, on the other, ensuring sufficient flexibility within direct payments packages to enable their clients to use their direct payments to meet wider needs than personal care.

- Care managers who had successfully worked with direct payments stressed the resulting sense of job satisfaction derived from empowering people to take back control over their lives and from seeing happier people as a result.

- Direct payments support services played a crucial role in enabling the older participants to enjoy direct payments.

- The level of funding of direct payments support services is sometimes based on historical precedents and budgetary constraints rather than on strategic decision making and recognition of different needs of different client groups. The absence of government guidelines results in wide variation in the level of funding between different local authority areas and, therefore, in the level and duration of support available to direct payments recipients.

Introduction

Direct payments were pioneered by the Disabled People's Movement and have been associated with better-quality support arrangements and higher levels of satisfaction for disabled people and cost-effectiveness for local authorities (Zarb and Nadash, 1994; Zarb, 1998).

Direct payments have the potential to revolutionise social care. They are based on the simple idea of giving disabled people money instead of services to meet assessed needs. This enables disabled people to "create and manage their own services" (Zarb, 1995, p 12) and to decide which forms of assistance to receive, and when, how and from whom. Assistance can be provided as and when needs arise, and is not tied to one location. This better enables disabled people to get on with the lives of their choosing. Direct payments are thus an important means of Independent Living (Hasler et al, 1999).

This does not mean, however, that giving cash instead of care is in itself enough to ensure greater choice and control for disabled people. Much depends upon how much flexibility local authorities grant disabled people in deciding how to meet their needs. A key factor here is the translation of a community care assessment into a direct payments package that retains that flexibility. Further, support services[1] that provide the information and assistance people want to set up their own services, and provide opportunities for peer support, are essential prerequisites for successful direct payments schemes (Hasler et al, 1998).

The opportunities provided by direct payments have now been extended to older people. This report examines how direct payments work for them.

We have chosen to use the term 'older people' rather than 'disabled people' in this report, even though some of our participants preferred to define themselves as 'disabled'. Our reason is that 'older people', along with other administrative categories such as 'physical disability', 'learning difficulties', 'mental health' and 'sensory impairment', is used by local authority social services departments (SSDs) to organise their budgets, staff and service resources for

---

[1] Direct payments support services have different names, for example, Personal Assistance Support Schemes and Independent/Integrated Living Schemes.

'adult' services. 'Older people' in this context means people aged 65 and over. Such categories are based more upon a pathology than a social model. Additionally, older people often face particular inequities relative to other user groups. These have historically included lower cost ceilings linked to the costs of residential care (Audit Commission, 1997), less innovative care packages, fewer community options, and inflexible and unresponsive services (SSI, 1998). These inequities demonstrate the lower priority accorded to older people's independence and social inclusion (Henwood, 2002). Tightening eligibility criteria have increased the focus upon risk at the expense of prevention, social participation and independence (Clark et al, 1998; Gorman and Postle, 2003). Budget allocation and services rarely reflect the recognition that older people have lifestyles or social lives of their own.

In short, social care provision for older people can be limited to minimal maintenance that assumes that they are passive and pays little regard to individuality, self-determination and choice.

Direct payments can change social care for older people just as it has done for younger disabled people. But making this a reality must involve challenging the notion that older people are passive recipients of social care and recognising that they can indeed 'create and manage their own services'. It also demands that SSDs appreciate the ethos of Independent Living that underpins direct payments.

Policy context

This chapter explains where direct payments have come from and gives an overview of some of the relevant policy developments. It is difficult to avoid the use of 'policy language' and so we must apologise if some readers find it jargon-laden. Reading this chapter is not essential but may be helpful in that the policy context is relevant to the context of the report.

The 1996 Community Care (Direct Payments) Act authorised local authorities to make cash payments in lieu of services to some people assessed as needing community care services. People over the age of 65 were initially excluded from the scope of the Act, but in February 2000 new regulations removed this inequity. The Act has also now been extended to younger people aged 16 to 18, 'informal' carers, and parents of disabled children.

The Act was originally permissive. However, new regulations effective from April 2003 impose an obligation on local authorities in England to offer direct payments to all those eligible for them.

In August 2002 the Department of Health issued a draft policy and guidance consultation paper to the Direct Payments Act (DoH, 2002a). The accompanying notes demanded an increase in the number of direct payments recipients, particularly older people, and indicated that this will be monitored.

There can be little doubt that extending direct payments is part of the modernising agenda for social care. The government regards direct payments as an important means towards promoting independence, increased choice and control, improved quality of life and social inclusion. It is investing £3 million per annum over three years to increase the number of people receiving direct payments (DoH, 2003a). In announcing the Direct Payments Development Fund, the Health Secretary stressed making direct payments a reality for "tens of thousands of older people" (Milburn, 2002).

The government's determination to ensure that older people have equal access to direct payments is in line with the policy agenda of rooting out age discrimination, as outlined in the *National service framework for older people* (NSF) (DoH, 2001a), and affirmed in *Fair access to care services* (FACS) (DoH, 2002b). However, other areas of age discrimination remain, including the exclusion of new applicants aged 66 and over from the Independent Living

Fund. This contributes to the inequity of lower-cost ceilings and runs counter to the government's agenda of rooting out age discrimination.

The flexibility offered by direct payments can also be extended to community healthcare. The 1999 Health Care Act enables local authorities and their NHS partners to provide joint or pooled budgets and to jointly contribute to a direct payment.

Precursors to direct payments

Since the 1980s, cash payments have been made under the auspices of the Independent Living Fund and indirect payments schemes operated by some local authorities. These, together with the growth of the Independent Living Movement in Britain and the negative experiences of disabled people receiving community care services, have been identified as contributing towards the introduction of direct payments (Glendinning et al, 2000).

The Independent Living Fund

The Independent Living Fund (ILF) was set up in 1988 as a result of pressure from disability organisations to compensate disabled people who lost out financially when Income Support replaced Supplementary Benefit. The ILF proved very popular with disabled people, who used the cash benefits to purchase the assistance they wanted; some of them thereby avoided admission to residential care. When it was introduced, the ILF had no upper age limit and was administered independently of local authorities.

The costs of the ILF escalated far beyond government expectations. In 1993 the government closed the original ILF fund to new applicants, and opened a new fund, the Independent Living 93 Fund, on a different basis. Disabled people can now newly access ILF monies only if they are receiving at least £200 of services per week from their local authorities – which shifts the power to local authorities. The maximum individuals can receive is £375 per week from the 93 Fund and, crucially, new applicants aged 66 and over are excluded.

Indirect payments

The numerous indirect payments schemes set up as the result of pressure from disabled people constituted another major precursor to direct payments.

Until the passing of the 1996 Act, making cash payments to disabled people in lieu of arranging services was illegal. From the 1980s, disabled people and local authorities circumscribed the legal obstacles to making cash payments to service users by setting up trusts or making payments through third-party organisations. These indirect payments schemes were widespread and typically operated no upper age limit.

The experiences of disabled people receiving cash instead of care compared favourably with the restrictions faced by those receiving directly provided services, adding impetus to the campaign for direct payments (Glendinning et al, 2000). Also, from the 1980s Centres for Independent Living were set up in Britain, which were crucial in the development of the principles and practice of Independent Living, including providing advice and support for disabled people recruiting and employing their own personal assistants (PAs).

Direct payments and older people

Older people were recipients of both indirect payments and original ILF payments, and successfully managed their own support arrangements. However, there were often crucial differences between, on the one hand, the monitoring and administrative demands of these schemes, what the payments could be used for and who could be employed, and, on the other, the conditions now attached to direct payments.

There seems little reason why older people should not also benefit from direct payments. However, very little is known about how direct payments will work for them. Studies in the UK are limited but suggest mixed attitudes to becoming employers of PAs (Zarb and Oliver, 1993), lack of knowledge about direct payments, and concerns about safety and the administrative demands (Barnes, 1997; Glasby and Littlechild, 2002).

Younger disabled people led the campaign for direct payments and the development of the Independent Living Movement. Direct payments are not generally well-known among older people, and until this changes it seems likely that demand for direct payments by older people will remain low. Yet there are encouraging signs that more older people are taking up direct payments. Statistics published by the Department of Health show that, for the period 2001-02, 1,100 people aged 65 and over were receiving direct payments – a substantial increase from the previous year's figure of 500 (DoH, 2003b).

Direct payments should enable older people to create and manage their own services to meet the needs they deem important. However, much depends again upon the level of payments they receive, the support available, and the flexibility they have in prioritising their own needs and how they will be met.

Fair Access to Care Services

Inequities between user groups may be addressed and rectified by *Fair access to care services* (FACS), at the heart of which is "the principle that councils should operate just one eligibility decision for all adults seeking social care support – namely, should people be helped or not" (DoH, 2002b, p 2).

This policy promises greater equity for older people but it remains to be seen whether practice and culture will follow. The new national eligibility framework introduced by FACS places emphasis upon 'risks to independence' and their prevention for all client groups. However, it also remains to be seen whether fundamental discriminatory assumptions about what independence means to older people will be challenged.

FACS focuses upon four factors as key to maintaining independence: autonomy, health and safety, managing daily routines, and involvement in family and community life. Much depends on how these factors are interpreted and balanced against each other. A focus upon safety might be at the expense of one on involvement, for example (Henwood, 2002), leaving older people little better-off than before.

Nevertheless, as Henwood (2002, p 83) says, FACS "could mark a significant step forward in conceptualising independence" by widening the base to include factors beyond safety and the ability to manage personal hygiene and nutrition.

Black and minority ethnic older people

The demand for culturally sensitive services for Black and minority ethnic people is a recurrent theme within government documents and guidelines and in Social Services Inspectorate reports (for example, DoH/SSI, 1998; SSI, 2000, 2002). The NSF and FACS are relevant in ensuring the equitable provision of person-centred services, while specific performance indicators cover assessment and service provision for minority ethnic people (DoH, 2002c). Furthermore, the 2000 Race Relations (Amendment) Act enforces the obligation of public bodies to ensure equal access to services and to promote race equality.

While direct payments should not be seen as a panacea filling gaps or making up deficiencies in provision and commissioning practices, they can be an innovative means for Black and minority ethnic older people to secure a culturally relevant service. Support services sensitive to the needs of Black and minority ethnic older people are an essential prerequisite to achieving this.

Local authority issues

The government intends to monitor the progress of local authority social services departments in giving older people access to direct payments, in part through a performance indicator. However, the extension of direct payments to older people coincided with a period of substantial and ongoing organisational and managerial changes, which may have impeded their progress. At the same time, culture and practice often lag behind policy, leaving "a gap between the rhetoric about independence and its implementation" (SSI, 2002, para.4.34).

Currently, local authority care managers are a primary source of information for older people about direct payments. Various studies (for example, Dawson, 2000; DoH/SSI, 2000) have noted 'gate-keeping', paternalism, reluctance, uncertainty, and a lack of confidence on the part of care managers in providing information on direct payments. Nevertheless, some local authorities have performed well and highlight the importance of 'champions' among care managers whose mind-sets extend beyond simply using traditional domiciliary services.

Finance and achieving increased capacity in the home care sector are two related issues facing local authorities. Current financing by central government is inadequate to achieve the necessary expansion of independent sector domiciliary provision (George, 2003). Direct payments may prove one of the ways in which SSDs can meet the shortfall in domiciliary provision in some parts of the country. If it is also recognised that direct payments are a means to achieve best value, then the advantages to local authorities are self-evident.

Willing and able

Local authorities can make direct payments only to people who are willing to receive them and who are able to manage them, alone or with assistance. The guidance document to direct payments (DoH, 2003c) makes clear that local authorities should adopt a positive stance when interpreting the 'willing and able' criteria. And, as Hasler et al (1999, p 39) say, "being 'willing' or 'able' are not fixed states" but are determined by the amount of support available to the individual. The role of direct payments support services is clearly paramount in providing information to ensure informed consent and necessary assistance to enable people to manage direct payments.

The importance of direct payments support services

It is now widely accepted, including in government guidance (DoH, 2003c), that a well-established support service is vital to the success of direct payments schemes. At the very least, support services should provide peer support, information, advice and/or advocacy and training (Hasler et al, 1999).

Support services may be provided by voluntary organisations, directly by social services departments, or by organisations of disabled people. Strong arguments have been made in favour of the last on the grounds that organisations of disabled people can provide peer support to other disabled people and create more effective partnerships between local authorities and disabled people as providers and users of services (Hasler et al, 1998; NCIL, 2002).

However, policy guidance does not stipulate who should provide the support function. Nor is there any guidance on the level of funding of support services by local authorities. This can mean wide variation between different local authority areas.

Some older people may prefer to receive this type of support from friends and family, but it needs to be a choice: that is to say, there must be alternatives. And it is important to ensure that handing over the control to informal carers does not totally dispossess older people of the choice and control that direct payments offer (Clark and Spafford, 2001). This poses a challenge to local authorities wanting to give older people access to direct payments *and* to adhere to the ethos of Independent Living underpinning direct payments.

The Direct Payments Development Fund may address some of the issues outlined in this chapter. It offers opportunities to develop sustainable partnerships between councils and the community and voluntary sector, innovative practices and new models of service delivery to improve awareness of, and access to, direct payments for older people and other under-represented groups.

3

The research

The research underpinning this report was conducted between January 2002 and July 2003 (for details of the research methods, see the Appendix). It explored how direct payments work for older people. Specifically, it examined the following areas:

- how older people find out about, choose, and make direct payments work for them;
- the perspective of care managers working with older people and their role in making direct payments work; and
- the role of direct payments support services in making direct payments work for older people.

Forty-one older people from three local authority areas (a City, a County and a Borough) who were in receipt of direct payments participated in the research, as did five senior managers, 32 care managers and 11 team managers, plus 10 direct payments support service workers from the various areas.

The older participants

Thirty-five white older people and/or their informal carers, who were receiving direct payments, together with six Black Somali older people, participated in the research. Fifteen of these older people were managing the scheme themselves with support from the direct payments support services (10 lived alone); the rest received varying degrees of support also from their partners, other family members and, in one instance, a neighbour. The older participants' ages ranged from the mid-60s to the early 90s.

We did not succeed in attracting older research participants experiencing mental health or learning difficulties. We believe that this probably reflects the fact that direct payments are rarely offered in these cases. It is nevertheless a major omission in terms of the research.

The local authorities

The three English local authorities participating in the research comprised an outer London borough (the Borough), a southern county (the County), and a northern city council (the City). The County was geographically widespread and contained urban, rural and coastal areas. Each local authority had a different type of direct payments scheme and/or different forms of direct payments support services.

The County and the Borough had long histories of making cash payments in lieu of care through indirect payments schemes, introduced thanks to the efforts of local disabled people.

The Borough

At the time of the research, 80 people, including 15 older people, were receiving payments through the Borough's Independent Living Scheme (ILS). The ILS had been an indirect payments scheme before the 1996 Community Care (Direct Payments) Act. Payments were made through a local organisation of disabled people, which later became a Centre for Independent Living (CIL). That scheme had no upper age limit. Since the 1996 Act, individuals had had the option of receiving their direct payments:

- directly from the local authority, or
- through the CIL.

All our participants, together with the vast majority of ILS recipients in the Borough, had chosen the latter.

The Borough discouraged the purchase of agency services with direct payments, for two reasons: first, VAT liability made this less cost-effective[2]; and second,

employing PAs rather than having care assistants employed by a third party was deemed to better fit the philosophy of Independent Living.

The CIL provided both the support and the monitoring functions, for which it received funding from the local authority, as well as to make the payments, pay the support workers and cover training costs. The CIL received care plans from care managers giving the assessed number of hours and the amounts of payments to be made.

The Borough paid three different hourly rates: standard, unsocial, and sleepover. Recruitment and administration costs, holiday and sickness pay, employers' National Insurance contributions, bank holiday pay, and so forth, were reimbursed through top-up monies.

The County

The County had one of the most successfully promoted direct payments schemes in the country. Of about 600 people on direct payments, 100 were older people. This probably stemmed from the County's earlier proactive stance in using Independent Living Transfer[3] to create a ring-fenced budget for its indirect payments scheme and to fund an

---

[2] From 31 January 2003 welfare services provided by state-regulated private welfare agencies have been exempt from VAT (see HM Customs and Excise, 2003).

[3] The Independent Living Transfer was a specific transfer of money that was related to the changes in community care and the closure of the Independent Living Fund in 1993. Although it was allocated as part of the Special Transitionary Grant (STG), its significance was that it was clearly labelled Independent Living and therefore provided the opportunity for local authorities to use it to promote Independent Living for disabled people (see Kestenbaum, 1995).

independent support worker to provide information and support to indirect payments users.

The County had two direct payments options in operation. In the first (Option A):

- individuals were allocated a set hourly rate inclusive of employers' National Insurance contributions, travel costs, holiday and sickness pay, insurance and administrative costs, and hourly rates of pay enhancement. This option was designed primarily for those wishing to employ PAs, though it could be used to purchase agency provision;
- people were not financially assessed: rather, the hourly rate was net of a client contribution.

The second option (Option B) was introduced in 1998 to offer a flexible hourly rate, generally for people who wanted to contract with an agency rather than employ their own PAs. The local authority paid the same hourly rate as it would had it directly purchased the service itself.

- Individuals were subject to a financial assessment and the same charging policy as direct service users.
- It was usual for individuals to purchase agency services, but the money could also be used for employing PAs.

The support service was accommodated by a CIL. The local authority undertook the monitoring function.

The City

The City first introduced direct payments following the 1996 Community Care (Direct Payments) Act, in response to pressure from disabled people's groups. In this scheme direct payments were paid at variable hourly rates: standard, evening/night/weekend, and sleepover. The payments could be used to employ PAs or purchase agency services. The same rates applied whichever option was chosen. Bank holiday supplements, sick and holiday pay, initial start-up costs and a contingency fund were paid annually into the individual's bank account.

The support service was in-house, that is, provided directly by social services. Although assessment by care managers was necessary to start the process of direct payments, the support service workers, known as Independent Living Advisers, implemented the 'willing and able' criteria and provided information and support.

The support service also provided an audit and payroll service and an external accountancy service that could set up bank accounts, issue cheques, deal with tax and National Insurance, and fill in monitoring forms. The accountancy service was costly, but was utilised when necessary to overcome barriers to people accessing direct payments. This included older Somali people. The costs were born by the fund holders: care management budgets devolved to area level. The monitoring function was separate from the support service's functions.

At the time of the research there were 14 older people on direct payments in the City (out of a total of 155), six of whom were Somali older people. Five more

Somali older people, interested in direct payments, were in the referral/assessment system. The Somali older people were refugees, and all women.

Funding direct payments and direct payments support services

Funding for direct payments and support services must be found from existing budgets. Other than the Development Fund already mentioned, there has been no additional funding from central government.

In the Borough, funding for both direct payments and the support service was from a single, centrally managed, domiciliary care budget for all adult user groups. The money for direct payments was held as a discrete budget within the domiciliary care budget, but there was sufficient flexibility to transfer money from the domiciliary care budget o the ILS pool.

In the County, the community care budget was split across the various adult client groups: 'physical disability', 'older people', 'learning difficulties', and so on, and then again into operational and strategic streams. All budgets were centrally managed. Direct payments packages were funded from the budget of the relevant client group. The support service was funded from the 'physical disability' strategic budget.

The City system was similar, but the budgets were devolved to area level and the funding of the support service came from the 'physical disability' staffing budget.

Each of these funding arrangements undoubtedly has advantages and drawbacks but, importantly, all three local authorities funded direct payments from mainstream budgets. Mainstream budgets have more flexibility than dedicated budgets and send a clear message that direct payments are a mainstream choice for everyone (DIG, 1996).

The City's and the County's use of a 'physical disability' budget to fund support services reflected the fact that direct payments had historically been an option predominantly for physically disabled adults under the age of 65.

The levels of funding for support services in the Borough and the County were also 'historical' rather than the product of strategic planning decisions. This will be discussed later in this report (Chapter 5).

4

Discovering and choosing direct payments[4]

Finding out about direct payments

Demand for direct payments among older people is related to the quality and accessibility of information about them.

Our older participants found out about direct payments from a variety of sources. Care managers were the single most common source of information. Other common sources included friends already receiving direct payments, care assistants, resource centre workers, community groups, public talks, hospital staff and district nurses. This created a 'demand' (older people requesting direct payments), but getting the information in the first place was rather haphazard. Many older people and their partners felt that their care managers might have told them about direct payments, or at least told them earlier:

> **"It is so important for us to know what is best for us from the beginning, not to wait until I collapse and go into hospital."**

Some interviewees remarked that direct payments needed to be better advertised; national and local radio was seen as a particularly useful way of doing this. They also suggested that information be posted in GP surgeries, in chiropody clinics, in churches and other places where older people meet. Ensuring primary health care professionals as well as social workers are well-informed was also suggested.

'Word of mouth' was also very important, and perhaps particularly so for minority ethnic older people facing literacy as well as language barriers.

Minority ethnic community centres and outreach workers were identified during the research as important sources of information about direct payments as well as filling a more general information gap between statutory agencies and minority ethnic communities. Links between community groups and direct payments support services were also cited as important.

---

[4] The names of all participants have been changed to protect confidentiality.

Choosing direct payments

There were two major reasons why our older participants chose direct payments:

- they wanted greater choice and control over support arrangements; and
- direct payments were their sole means of getting the support required.

Wanting greater choice and control

The majority of our older participants wanted more choice and control over their support arrangements than could be offered by directly provided services, of which some participants had had negative experiences. Care assistants from in-house home care and independent agencies were, it was said, "too rushed" and often didn't stay for the full time allocated. Worries about who would come and indeed "whether they'd turn up at all" had caused some of our participants sleepless nights. Complaints were made that the agency never sent "the same person twice", which meant always having to explain what needed doing and how.

A worrying issue to emerge from our discussions was that the older people could feel "too frightened" to complain directly to their care assistants in case they "got annoyed and just went" or that nobody would come. The way that care assistants could treat you was described as "very scary" as "they can make your life a misery". Complaining to the care assistant could also lead to a reprimand by the agency. One woman who had experienced this told us:

"It takes away your dignity.... You feel like that you are not anymore a 60-odd years-old woman, but a child."

Other older people simply felt dispossessed of their homes:

"You didn't feel as though you were in your own home. You felt as though like, they were in charge."

Direct payments were attractive to many because they enabled them to determine how things were done. Sometimes couples saw this as ensuring the quality of support for the disabled partner as well as easing the strain on the care-giving partner. Sometimes it was to be physically handled in the preferred way:

"I knew that if I employed my own staff, they would have to do it the way I wanted it done, which I think is important."

Direct payments could also help overcome some people's reluctance to accept help. They feared they would lose control over their lives but direct payments meant they felt that they were "running things" rather than have "somebody else running it for me". Determining their routines was important in this.

The only way to get the support required

Direct payments were the only way that some older people could secure the particular sort of support that was required.

Mr Cox organised support for his neighbour, Miss Essex, through a broker agency that provided full-time live-in carers on a rota basis. He doubted social services' ability to organise 24-hour support using local agencies and to sustain the daily level of input to deal with issues arising for the care workers.

Miss Dixon's case was complex but she believed that direct payments were the only way for her to obtain the 'social care' support she required. Her needs straddled the health and social care domains. The health authority's nursing agency service did not meet Miss Dixon's requirements, nor were the nursing staff happy in providing personal care (which they saw as a social care domain). The social services department and health authority were also unable to agree on their respective responsibilities for long-term funding. Miss Dixon's care manager saw direct payments as a solution to the problem. Miss Dixon readily agreed, having been using her own savings to purchase her support and relying heavily on her sister, who lived with her. She would have liked the primary care trust to contribute to her direct payments but had been unsuccessful in securing this.

Direct payments were undoubtedly the sole means by which the Somali participants could find workers who spoke their language. Statutory and independent agencies in the City simply didn't have Somali-speaking care assistants. However, it was expected that this might change as some younger Somali women working as PAs had expressed interest in also working in home-care agencies.

Consultation with older people

Local authorities are reminded in the guidance to direct payments of the need to consult different user groups about local arrangements for direct payments schemes (DoH, 2003c). The importance of involving older people in partnership and consultation was recognised by local authority senior managers. It was simply not known how to achieve this where few older people were involved in user-led organisations, or where existing groups were either organisations *for* older people or carers' organisations. The Borough support service's proposed initiative in facilitating smaller peer support groups of older direct payments users may provide one useful model which could provide feedback into policy and practice development.

Nationally, there are now over 1,000 older people receiving direct payments. These older people have a wealth of experience of direct payments. Local authorities and direct payments support services could draw upon and utilise this resource to the benefit of other older people considering and taking up direct payments.

5

Using direct payments to employ personal assistants

Using direct payments can involve tasks ranging from recruiting, employing and managing PAs to keeping a separate bank account, keeping records, making financial returns, and complying with employment law in relation to payments and staff. Nothing in the guidance to direct payments decrees that individuals must manage this alone; in fact, this would be contrary to the whole ethos of direct payments. What is crucial is that the individual is in control of their support arrangements.

Given the scepticism about older people's willingness and ability to undertake these tasks, with or without support, it is important to examine how older people manage them.

The majority of our participants used their payments to employ PAs. Finding PAs was almost universally cited as a problem, as it is by other user groups (see, for example, Vasey, 2000). However, it can be particularly difficult for people who have only a small number of hours of employment to offer.

The four major ways of recruiting PAs were as follows:

- going on personal recommendation;
- advertising;
- employing through lists held by the direct payments support service; and
- employing former care assistants.

Nine people had recruited staff by putting up postcards in shops or post offices. However, the older people generally expressed a preference for recruiting via personal recommendation where this was possible.

Where advertising was necessary, there was a general preference to advertise locally so that distance and transport would not become an issue. As many participants pointed out, they could offer only limited hours of employment and therefore travel would be a disincentive for potential employees. This was most marked among those living in rural areas.

> **"I write out a postcard, try to vary what I put and put them in the local post office. I put them in all the local villages within a five-mile radius."**

A further advantage of advertising locally was that questions could be asked about applicants, thereby introducing an element of personal recommendation.

Nevertheless, sometimes a conscious decision was made to recruit from further afield. Indeed, this was seen to be a very positive option for one woman who didn't want anyone local to know about the sensitive nature of her needs.

Mr Dobson got round the problem of having too few hours to make employment worthwhile for potential employees by 'sharing' his PAs with a friend.

Miss Turner advertised in the local university for some of her PAs. She said the pay she could offer was "quite good" for students. Furthermore, if anything went wrong she could simply contact the university. She also advertised in a nearby hospital for PAs to help her with more intimate tasks such as bathing. The nurses she recruited were "very reliable" and, importantly,

> **"They're used to bathing people all the time … they know how to take you out and put you in the bath."**

The wording of the advert was important and needed careful consideration. One person successfully recruited a number of PAs using very personal wording. Another told us that she avoided using the term 'personal assistant' or 'PA' in the advertisement as this could mislead potential candidates into thinking it was a secretarial job.

Four people tried advertising in their local job centres, though only one was successful. A couple of people told us

that they were not allowed to state they wanted a mature person as this was deemed discriminatory.

Five people in the Borough recruited some of their PAs using a register maintained by the support service. They expressed an appreciation of the register, as this was deemed a relatively safe way of recruiting people.

Several older people had 'poached'[5] their staff from care agencies because they "already knew what their capabilities were".

In the majority of instances, employing former care assistants worked well. However, in one case the PAs failed to adapt to their new role as employees of the older person. Mrs Smith told us that she had a couple who were "taking over" and "telling me what to do and what not to do". This impeded Mrs Smith's perception of herself as the employer, until she decided to dismiss them.

The Somali older women had few problems in finding PAs. They recruited younger women from their own communities and on the recommendation of other community members. Mrs Raja, for example, told us:

> **"I ask the people … I say I need a nice lady whose care will do me well."**

The qualities that they looked for were kindness, willingness and respectfulness.

---

[5] In fact, most PAs who had been 'poached' retained their agency employment as well.

Restrictions on employing close relatives

A few participants felt it unfair that they couldn't use their direct payments to pay relatives. Usually this was to do with help going shopping or pursuing social activities. Mrs Ward, though, told us that she would like to be able to employ her daughter to provide her personal assistance. Her daughter had worked for a local care agency and had the requisite skills.

The older Somali participants, on the other hand, were emphatically opposed to employing relatives. They said they would have no redress if things went wrong, that it could create unwanted tensions, and

> **"... they might not do exactly what we want because we know each other."**

The Somali women felt that family members would think they "were the boss" instead of being employees. Overall it was felt that employing "outside people" was better.

Nevertheless, restrictions on employing family members may have been a barrier for some older people. Yet the new regulations extend the discretion of local authorities to allow, in exceptional circumstances, the employment of co-resident family members as well as those living in other households

References and interviews

Good references were generally seen as important for those who recruited through advertising, although some "trusted to luck" or simply based their decision upon whether or not they liked the person.

When interviewing, a few older people looked for specific skills in their PAs (for example, computer literacy, the ability to drive, or a 'good back' for lifting). But generally, companionability, compatibility, honesty, foresight, directness, and respect for the older person's self, home and belongings were at the top of most people's recruitment criteria. Some preferred to have PAs who had "dealt with disabled people in their careers" or who had some nursing skills. Others were wary of this, preferring to train their PAs themselves and ensure that they did not employ people who thought "they know it all before they start".

Most people presented a list of duties and requirements to their potential PAs at interviews, whereas others preferred to leave 'the what and the when' open.

The desire for openness and reciprocity was seen as very important in making the relationship work:

> **"Well, I said to both my girls when they first came on the scene, 'We're all grown ups here, and if I don't particularly like something that you've done, I will tell you. But at the same time, I expect you to be direct with me as well'.... Because that way it works fine."**

Any other skills a potential PA might have such as hairdressing or being able to sew or do massage were obvious, although not essential, advantages.

The majority of our older participants employed two or more PAs, mostly to ensure cover during absences but also sometimes to keep their PAs' income below the tax and National Insurance (NI) threshold. Some people avoided dealing with tax and NI, and indeed with contracts of employment, by engaging PAs on a self-employed basis; but this could take some selling during interviews.

Employing a number of PAs with a limited allocation of assessed hours could reduce the flexibility older people would otherwise want. Weekend support was also difficult to acquire, and sometimes older people had to pay extra out of their own pockets.

Permission to work

One of our older participants pointed to their vulnerability to prosecution if they inadvertently employed an asylum seeker without a work permit. Her perception was that the Job Centre failed to adequately check such matters, so putting "the responsibility on people like us". Direct payments support services may need to consider this sensitive issue.

Managing PAs

Relationships

The majority of our discussions on managing PAs centred on relationships. For most participants, handling the relationship with PAs was one, if not the most important, key to successfully managing direct payments. Most indicated that the relationship was friendly and for some mirrored extended family relationships. This was seen as working better than more "dictatorial"

management styles, of which, indeed, several were very critical:

"The days of domestic service are long since gone."

It also paid to have friendly relationships with PAs: PAs didn't mind doing extra while older employers reciprocated by listening to their PAs' problems, showing concern, and being flexible when family and personal issues occasionally caused lateness or absence.

Most employers otherwise successfully maintained the boundary between business and friendship, although a few said that they sometimes forgot that they were employers.

One of the most commonly mentioned issues for the older participants was that the relationship took place in their own homes. The home symbolises the private sphere of personal relationships and stands in contrast to the public sphere of the more impersonal. Many of our older participants had managerial or supervisory career backgrounds, which they said helped them now as employers. However, they also felt that there was a difference between past experiences and the present. Mrs Robinson articulated the point most clearly. She had, in her past career, been responsible for 16 staff "which I engaged and fired". That, however, was

"... a very different relationship, because that was a professional relationship. Here, they are in our home, they are sharing our lives. That was sharing my work."

By contrast, Mr Dobson wanted to maintain a strictly employment relationship with his PAs, although they tried, he said, to develop a friendship. He was keen to avoid the situation in which PAs felt that they could "come into the home and do whatever without bothering to enquire ... what's to be done":

"They try to take over ... it is a very big problem."

Others felt that being friendly and having a chat with the PAs was part of the benefits of direct payments, especially as they could choose a companionable person in the first place. Indeed, Mrs Fox told us she had had to let one PA go because she was "a bit officious" and "didn't really want to mix". She was pleased with the standard of work but felt the relationship didn't "gel somehow", which made it "a bit awkward".

The Somali participants told us that their PAs accorded them the respect they would their own mother. The older women were clearly "the boss" but combined this with a friendly and mutually respectful relationship with their PAs:

"I have got a lot of respect from my carer, but I have for my carer too.... It depends also on how we understand each other. Sometimes you can be friends and sometimes it's just boss."

The older women were aware that some of their PAs wanted to work for home care agencies, and so needed good references:

"Because they think they might get a good future ... they might think if they broke the

agreement they might not get a good report."

Sometimes, however, the problems involved in finding PAs could weaken the older person's position as an employer. For example, Mrs Anderson felt that some of the difficulties she had experienced with previous PAs stemmed from her "not keeping their nose to the grindstone". She was also wary of upsetting her PAs in case they decided:

"I'm not going to work for her. I'm just being treated like a slave."

It is clearly not easy for everyone to be an employer, particularly when the PAs work in the employer's home and it is hard to find employees. There were indications sometimes that older people would benefit from peer support in being employers. Nevertheless, the majority had and made good use of transferable skills that enabled them to manage the employment relationship in ways that best suited their preferences and requirements.

Managing cover during holidays and sickness

In many instances PAs working for the same person organised cover between themselves, and most employers were appreciative of this.

Having more than one PA clearly made it easier to arrange cover during holidays; it also helped when a PA became ill. Often in such instances the older person simply contacted another PA to ask them if they could cover. However, problems could arise.

Individuals who paid for more hours than they were assessed for also then had to subsidise holiday and sickness pay. Some older people avoided these issues by engaging self-employed PAs:

> **"I mean, if you insist on them as self-employed, it gets you out of the holiday situation."**

Some, however, did give holiday pay to self-employed PAs. As one said:

> **"I think if you've got good people, you've got to look after them."**

The Somali participants each employed just one PA. Most were new to direct payments and only one had had to deal with issues arising from their PA's absence. In this instance, Mrs Talpur's PA found "somebody nice" to replace her during her holiday.

Using direct payments to purchase agency services

Those participants who purchased agency services rather than engaging PAs gave as the primary reason for this choice not having to worry about finding cover for holidays and sick leave. As one woman caring for her husband said:

"I just haven't the time. I'm still very, very, busy, even as it is."

Most participants choosing this option were informal carers. Some were facing a crisis and wanted to get support arranged as soon as possible. Personal recommendation from someone that they trusted was important in choosing an agency. Cost was also an issue:

"It was primarily governed by cost, and of course I had to look at the abilities of the people they had. And I found that this one had people that were able and would fit within the budget so I had to make do with their carers ... but there are very few agencies that are able to supply the type of care we needed."

On the other hand, some older people were prepared to pay a bit more. Mrs Fields, for example, purchased agency services because she did not "want to be bothered" with "all that paperwork". Her payments did not quite cover the costs. She knew she could find a cheaper agency but having somebody she could trust was more important to her.

In the absence of personal recommendation, choosing an agency was not an easy task and there appeared to be little help or support available. One person told us that it was:

"... a lot of hit and miss, because it takes a lot of getting it right."

The agency option worked well for most who chose it. However, one man experienced difficulties over consistency and reliability of care assistants. Furthermore, his direct payments did not cover the costs and he went "into the red". In view of the difficulties, the care manager suggested he take on PAs instead. This was a much better arrangement.

Mr Griffiths also experienced problems with some care assistants who, he said, could not "hack" the intimate tasks involved in caring for his wife and who then tended "to walk". However, as he pointed out:

**"[Agencies] have to come up
with somebody straight away,
because I'm paying them the
money. So you don't have that
worry."**

Four non-resident informal carers
organised live-in care through broker
agencies. The agencies provided workers
on a rota basis; each typically stayed for
two weeks at a time. The agency charged
a fee for its services, which also included
dealing with tax, National Insurance and
employer's liability insurance. The
workers' salaries and travelling costs were
paid directly by the older people or
informal carers. Neither the agencies nor
the workers were local. Having workers
with no local connections was seen as a
distinct advantage, as they wouldn't be
"popping out to visit friends" or inviting
others back to the older person's home.

Restrictions and flexibility in the use of direct payments

Direct payments fit well into the policy agenda of promoting Independent Living, quality of life and social inclusion. Direct payments should empower people to determine and meet their personal and practical support needs on a daily basis, to enable them, as one participant put it, "to live a normal life". What a normal life involves must depend upon the individual, who is best placed to decide his or her priorities and how to achieve them within the available resources.

For Mr Clarke, living a normal life was about having PAs to take

"… a lot of work off my wife, and I'm pleased that I'm not sitting there like a cabbage."

He took control of his own support arrangements and, while his wife went on her own chosen holiday, was able to go on a fishing trip, accompanied by his PA. Going on holiday with his wife is "not a break for her ... she's still got to do for me". He paid the PA £100 for three nights away and 24-hour care. He had to put in extra of his own money to cover the costs, but as he said:

"It's brilliant, it beats staying in an old people's home. But you

see, you'd be paying about £170 for an old people's home. Well, we couldn't afford it."

Mr Clarke simply used his personal assistance outside of, rather than solely within, the home; and this was cheaper, as well as a lot more enjoyable, than traditional respite.

Mrs Young used her personal assistance to pursue her life-long interest in the arts. She still got "a buzz" out of this. She had to pay for her PA's additional costs – meals, petrol, and so on – out of her own pocket.

These two examples show how some older people want to go out and enjoy life. However, to do so they have to squeeze as much as they can from their direct payments, "jiggling the money around", sometimes having less than their allocated hours per week, and adding their own money to enhance the package. Creative usage of direct payments would otherwise be impossible, as Mr Clarke said, given their focus upon "personal care only" and the relatively small number of hours usually allocated to older people.

Mrs Evans used her hours primarily for domestic, rather than personal, assistance.

One hour per week was specifically allocated for hairdressing. In her case, as with several other couples, her husband helped her with intimate tasks, as this was her preference. It made it easier for her to do as much as possible for herself while retaining personal privacy:

"We have kept our physical selves to ourselves for the time being."

Mrs Evans didn't want her husband to have to do the housework as well, but was concerned that the County was "moving away from allowing the domestic". Mrs Evans's weekly hours had already been reduced to 13 (from 17), and she was worried about the future because a clean and tidy home was very important to the couple. Mrs Evans told us that she had always been proud of her home, and Mr Evans added:

"We don't like friends and relatives coming in and thinking we've got a dirty house."

The issue of housework was important to other couples where one of the partners was providing a lot of support for the other. Mr Fontwell, for example, had been allocated five hours per week for personal care. The couple purchased their support from an agency, but Mrs Fontwell paid for an extra hour each day to prevent her husband from being hurried and to get some domestic help. Without that, she said, she would be "playing catch-up all day", which was "wearing".

Having this extra hour meant that Mrs Fontwell was better able to care for her husband. Yet there was no indication that she had been assessed and offered direct

payments, as may have been her right under the 2000 Carers and Disabled Children Act, the policy guidance to which makes clear that carers might use their payments to secure, for example, domestic assistance (DoH, 2001b).

In fact, we came across no partners or other informal carers who had been offered direct payments in their own right. Our interviews with care management teams indicated little awareness of this option. A senior manager also told us that domestic assistance was not an eligible need, even for informal carers.

A carer's assessment had, however, been suggested to the partner of another of our participants. Mrs Fox told us that her husband's "back problems" meant he could no longer "do what he used to do for me". She said that social services wanted to assess her husband "for looking after me". This confused the couple:

"Because I'm the one on direct payments, it should be me being assessed for needing further hours, because he's no longer my main carer."

'Health' versus 'social care' needs

There were restrictions upon what direct payments can be used for. Chiropody and physiotherapy were not allowed as these were deemed to be 'health' rather than social care needs.

Mrs Evans's medical condition was such that her nails were very brittle and breakage could easily cause infection. Mr Evans did not feel confident to cut his wife's nails. Nevertheless, they did not feel it "quite right" to surreptitiously pay for chiropody with their direct payments as "feet are not in the formula". Mrs Evans did think it rather absurd that

"… they allow me to have my hair washed, but I can't have my toenails cut!"

However, older people got their PAs to cut their nails, and one had her husband's PAs trained to undertake physiotherapy with him.

However, there were circumstances where PAs could not be used to fulfil such needs. Mrs Anderson, for example, would have liked permission to use her direct payments for her hydrotherapy, without which, she said, "I couldn't do what I do now".

There were no instances in the research in which local and health authorities had used the flexibilities introduced in the 1999 Health Act, which enables health authorities to contribute to joint direct payments packages and, in partnership with local authorities, to jointly form ring-fenced budgets for specified services or user groups. The use of PAs to meet some healthcare needs amounts to a de facto shunting of costs from health authorities to local authorities through the mechanism of direct payments (Glendinning et al, 2000).

8

Managing the money

As has been indicated, the money allocated to older people through direct payments was not always sufficient to cover the costs of their personal assistance or agency cover, and the older person had to put in extra. Similarly, the exclusion of needs deemed 'health'-related rather than 'social' meant that these had to be separately financed unless a PA could provide them.

However, some older people accumulated excess monies in their direct payments accounts. Miss Turner, for example, had paid transport costs out of her own money, although she was entitled to use her payments for this. She had decided to be

> **"careful of their money, and not go splash, splash, splash.... I've been just saving it up for a rainy day, in case anything bad happens."**

Miss Turner fell foul of the Borough's policy, to the effect that accumulated monies in excess of 5% of the individual's total annual allocation should be clawed back.

The problem illustrated by Miss Turner's experience is perhaps that older people

were not always aware that saving from their direct payments for a rainy day was self-defeating. Not only could they indirectly lose their own money, but there was also the danger that care managers might reduce their hours in the belief that they were getting more than they needed.

Yet money could accumulate simply because it could take a while to employ someone, or to purchase services if the older person did not already have someone in mind. This happened to a number of our participants who, nevertheless, went without some of the things they needed because of the restrictions upon the use of the payments.

At the opposite end of the scale, situations could arise in which delays in local authority processing of direct payments led to the accumulation of excess money. Mr Fowler told us that his allocated hours had been substantially increased, but "it took them a month to do it" and his payment was then backdated. However, Mr Fowler had been unwilling to spend this in advance in case the local authority "changed its mind". As a result, Mr Fowler accumulated an excess in his account.

Managing on the money

Some of our older participants, particularly in the County, felt that the hourly rate they received was inadequate, pointing out that either they topped up the money themselves or paid their PAs peanuts.

A survey conducted in the County by a disabled people's organisation found that many direct payment users were paying more per hour than their direct payments allowed. That standard hourly rates can ignore variations *within* local authority areas perhaps contributed to this.

It also seemed that older people in those local authorities that made separate payments through top-up monies or separate annual payments were better able to cover costs incurred for recruitment and so forth, and to keep these monies distinct from those intended for paying PAs.

Older people incurred additional costs when they had PAs accompany them on outings or, in some cases, on holiday. These included meals and other living costs and, in exceptional cases, theatre or cinema tickets. These hidden costs were not taken into account when the hourly rates of direct payment were determined.

Sliding scales

A number of our participants operated sliding pay scales for their PAs, according to their experience and the type of work they did. Some explicitly recommended this to make the money go further and absorb the some of the hidden costs. This did not work for everybody,

however, and some were still out of pocket.

Independent Living 93 Fund

People aged 66 years and over are excluded from applying to the Independent Living 93 Fund. This is discriminatory and neglects the dual impact of impairment and ageing:

> **"It costs you more to be older and impaired. I mean just to be older it costs you money, but to be impaired as well, you need more money."**

A number of our participants had aged with a disability but had managed up to and beyond retirement age without statutory support services. They were now excluded from the 93 Fund.

Others had managed to access Independent Living Fund monies before they were 66, and it was only through these that they were they able to afford the support they needed.

The upper age limit of the ILF is a factor in the inequity of lower cost ceilings for older clients, which increases older people's vulnerability to residential care. It was small wonder our older participants felt fortunate if they got ILF monies; it is unacceptable that they needed to feel so.

> **"We are just so fortunate that we hooked into the ILF. If we couldn't hook into that, we would have been in trouble."**

9

Meeting the administrative and financial demands

Bank accounts

Direct payments must be kept in a separate bank or building society account used only for that purpose. With few exceptions, this created no problems, and for one man was a good idea because "it doesn't get mixed up with your own money then". Some people did find it "a bit of a nuisance", however.

Mrs Amos's parents were both on direct payments, and each had to have a separate account. Mrs Amos had enduring power of attorney and looked after all her parents' financial affairs, including managing their direct payments. Having to deal with two accounts increased her work.

Other informal carers with enduring power of attorney pointed out that, while they could sign cheques relating to the direct payments account, they could not have "a plastic card" to withdraw cash. This made it extremely difficult for them to make cash payments. Mr Cox paid his neighbour's live-in agency carers by cheque but they also needed cash sometimes, particularly when they were travelling home. Mr Cox was unable to

draw this cash without going to a major branch of the bank some miles away.

Some of our older participants, as stated, needed to subsidise their direct payments with their own money to cover their costs. This could lead to difficulties if, as Mrs Fox did, they put that extra amount into their direct payments account to cover the cheques. She now has to go through her account and put it right. Yet, as she told us:

> **"Now if I take out all the bits that I've put in, I'm going to be bankrupt on that account. So I'm having to speak to somebody about it."**

In the City, all the Somali participants and one white British participant used the accountancy service linked to the direct payments support service.

Certainly, having to deal with the banking and other financial, payroll and audit functions demanded of direct payments recipients would have been too great a barrier to the older Somali participants. None of the women spoke English, and some found real difficulties in dealing with things like bills and official letters.

Tax, National Insurance and employers' liability insurance

Very few of our older participants had to deal with tax and National Insurance, since the majority had PAs whose income was below the threshold or who were self-employed.

Mr Fowler was among the minority who did have to deduct tax and National Insurance contributions. He had realised "too late" that he could have had his PAs on a self-employed basis. He got in touch with the local tax office "for new business people", who gave him the necessary advice and instructions. Mr Fowler found it difficult for the first couple of months, but not overwhelmingly so because of past business experience.

Miss Dixon also had employees who were liable to pay tax and National Insurance. She handed this over to an accountant to deal with because, like many others, she would not have known "where to start".

In one of our areas we noticed that some PAs worked for several older people. The older people were concerned about who was responsible for ensuring the Inland Revenue was informed. Older people with self-employed PAs were similarly unclear about their responsibilities. It seemed that this was an area requiring further attention and clear advice for older people.

There was also an issue with insurance. While many had taken out employers' liability insurance, others who were reliant upon their household insurance were very concerned about whether this would provide adequate cover in the

event of a claim. It was unclear how the Somali older participants dealt with such issues, and this may indicate the need for a more systematic approach to advice on employer responsibility.

Managing the paperwork

Many of our older participants had help with the paperwork, from partners, relatives, friends or PAs. The paperwork was seen as quite overwhelming, at least initially. Those with transferable skills from previous careers and occupations saw them as a distinct advantage. Support services were also deemed vital here. However, some older people faced particular difficulties.

Mrs Black felt that insufficient account was taken of the impact of specific forms of impairment on the person's physical ability to fill in the forms:

> **"You know they lump us all together as though we've all got the same disability, but we haven't."**

In her case, completing her quarterly returns was difficult and time-consuming because of impairment to her hands. Mrs Black's comments reflect the difficulties some other older people faced in dealing with the paperwork. For example, people with visual impairments pointed to the importance of ensuring that all information and advice on direct payments be produced in different formats, including Braille.

Informal carers could also find the paperwork overwhelming, particularly when they were struggling to combine this with caring for their loved ones. Mrs

Campbell had initially refused direct payments because she felt "absolutely over-loaded" and couldn't "begin to get my head round this". She simply wanted to get through each day. Her dissatisfaction with agency services led her to reconsider. She purchased the services of another agency and, although it cost more than her direct payment, she avoided the "hassle" of being an employer. However, she had never "done the audit". She was concerned that the local authority would sanction her and that the support service worker, who had visited twice to explain, would think her

"... a complete nincompoop.... Because I still don't understand it."

Value of direct payments to older people

It would be difficult to overstate the value our older participants attached to direct payments. The degree of consistency between what the older people said and what is reported in other studies of younger people and direct payments is remarkable. Glendinning et al. (2000, p 17), for example, point to the psychological benefits accruing from the "enhanced choice, continuity and control offered by direct payments" for younger disabled people and to the related social, emotional and physical health benefits. These findings were reflected in this research. There is a distinct 'added value' to direct payments which reflects, for these older people, much of the ethos of current government policy on social care, quality and independence.

Mrs Robinson told us that direct payments had "revolutionised" her life

"... because you are in control of what you have done."

Direct payments enabled Mr and Mrs Robinson to direct their support to achieving the things important to their quality of life. Mr Robinson was now, for example, able to watch an evening football match without being put into bed before the end of the match, while Mrs

Robinson had her "home ticking over so that it's comfortable".

There is, of course, a huge debate on what constitutes quality of life. But, as Harding (1997, p 3) points out, quality of life depends in part on "'social health' – keeping up one's interests, friendships and participation in society". These are the things that make "life worth living" and have beneficial effects on physical, mental and emotional health.

Quality of life might be seen as the 'happiness factor'. Certainly, this was the case for many. Mrs Ward told us that "I'm more happy on it" and that she had got a "new lease of life" such that she felt she could physically "do more", had "more go" and could "go out a lot more" than she used to.

For those who required assistance to go out, having PAs was crucial to maintaining quality of life.

Mrs Young described direct payments as "marvellous, like a magical door opening". She had felt "suicidal" being "stuck in that flat all the time". What she really wanted was someone to take her out. She used some of her payments to employ a PA/driver to take her to art exhibitions. Being 'stuck in the flat' also meant that she had to live with the dust, which depressed her further. Another PA kept the flat tidy, though "you can't look in the corners".

Others told us how much they enjoyed outings with their PAs. Some, like Mrs Ungerson, were enabled to retain her personal identity and family and social roles. Being able to go out with her PA to buy Christmas and birthday cards and presents, and choosing outfits for social outings with her husband, were crucial in this.

Several older participants reported feeling more relaxed since receiving direct payments, and having more choice and more freedom, which enabled them to do so much more. Some particularly enjoyed being able to choose people they liked and therefore having someone they could talk to, as this was something they otherwise missed.

All of our Somali participants stressed that they felt happier since being able to purchase their own support through direct payments. Their family relationships had improved as they no longer "moaned" at their children to help them. Mrs Osmani told us that she had left "all the anger with my family behind", which meant everyone was happier and

"... now I am calm. I feel like I am doing the thing on my [own]."

For Mrs Hassani and Mrs Soomoo, having their own workers enhanced their feelings of safety. That her PA collected her pension removed Mrs Hassani's "worry of being mugged". For Mrs Soomoo, having

her door locked at night was important, as was the cup of tea in the morning.

Having help with shopping was particularly important for the Somali women because the language barrier often made it difficult for them to observe their cultural norms:

"Sometimes I don't understand. I will [...] choose some food that I don't eat. I get confused and end up eating something with alcohol or pork which we cannot eat, by mistake."

Direct payments enabled the older Somali participants to secure culturally relevant services – which many local authorities still struggle to achieve. Having PAs who spoke their language was, they said, crucial but additionally, like our other older participants, they were in control and could determine what their PAs did for them.

There can be no doubt that relationships with PAs, the roles they performed under the direction of the older person, the choice and flexibility offered by direct payments, and the 'respect' afforded to being the employer were all decisive in enhancing the quality of life of our older participants.

Direct payments were crucial to enabling some older people to remain in their own homes. This was particularly the case with those older people who required 24-hour support, but also for a small number who felt so unhappy with directly provided services that they had been considering moving into residential care.

The age divide

Moving from adult to older persons' services

As already noted, 'older people' is one of the administrative categories used by social services (and other statutory agencies) to organise their budgets, staffing and service resources. Historically, fewer resources have been allocated to older people than to younger adult groups, while community options for social participation have been more limited.

These are clearly examples of overt age discrimination that should be tackled by government policy initiatives such as Fair Access to Care Services and the National Service Framework for Older People. However, it may be more difficult to root out less overt discriminatory perceptions around the presumed lifestyles of older people and what older people need to maintain their independence and quality of life.

Moving from adult to older persons' services

Some of the issues around resources were thrown into sharp relief by the experiences of those participants making the transition between adult and older persons' services.

Mrs Ward had been disabled for many years when she crossed the administrative boundary. She told us about her new care manager:

"Well she keeps on about old people you see and because I'm 65 I suppose I am old, but I don't class myself as old."

Mrs Fox, like a number of others, found it "disconcerting" that she no longer had a named care manager but had to take "pot luck". Furthermore, at her review time she was visited by a care manager who "didn't know anything about me, and she didn't know anything about direct payments either".

Some of the older people crossing this boundary were worried that their hours might be reduced. Mrs Fox said her previous social worker had told her that, when she moved over to the older persons' team, they would reassess her:

"... and it would be they who decided if I needed the hours that I'm having, or not. And I was very frightened about that."

In fact, two participants had their hours reduced when they reached 65, although one had them reinstated at a subsequent review. They believed this to be part of a more general "squeeze" in the local authorities. It is counter to current government legislation to reduce hours on the basis of age; this can happen only if the person's needs change. However, it may be that what counts as a need has become age-specific.

At the same time, it is also clear that what counts as a need is budget- and resource-driven (Gorman and Postle, 2003). Indeed, in one local authority area budgets were so tight that systematic reviews of care packages were being undertaken with a view to reducing as many as possible. Small wonder that some of our participants were frightened of contacting social services when they felt they needed more hours, in case they were reduced.

A major shortfall for older people was said to lie in accessing resources for social and leisure facilities. This was seen to emanate from budgetary constraints, and the history of inequitable commissioning practices that have led to fewer community options for older people.

Older people wanting or being deemed to require social outlets were generally pointed towards day-centre provision, while respite care was often equated with having a holiday. Some older people were able to use their direct payments to meet their social and leisure needs in other ways. Care managers were often aware of this but felt unable to make it an explicit part of a care plan, believing that their line managers would not endorse it.

Day centres and holidays

Day and resource centres had age thresholds which our participants felt were discriminatory. Disabled people who attended day and resource centres found that, because of the age thresholds, they had to move over to day centres for older people when they reached 65. Budget constraints in older persons' services also meant that they were not able to attend as many times a week as before. There were also reported restrictions on help from social services in securing funding for holidays.

Mrs Ward fell foul of both the day centre and holiday issues when she reached 65. She was told that she would have to attend a day centre for older people and it was made clear that holidays would take the form of respite rather than going on group holidays with other disabled people. Mrs Ward was in fact given an extension of five years for both. Her care manager described this as a transition period, during which time Mrs Ward was

"... meant to be adapting to the lifestyle of an older person."

The idea that people need to "adapt [...] to the lifestyle of an older person" has wider resonance than the direct payments scenario. It comes from an ageist approach to social care work with older people. It also reflects the fragmented approach whereby services continue to be designed and provided separately for older people and disabled people. In effect, Mrs Ward ceased to be a disabled person because the focus was on her age. This ignored her needs as a disabled person because provision was service-driven. Care managers who operate as

Mrs Ward's did are condoning the service-
driven and ageist nature of this provision.

The type of attitude articulated by this
care manager, combined with restricted
resources for older people, does not
augur well for the potential of direct
payments to promote quality of life, social
inclusion and independence for older
people.

In the Borough, consideration is being
given to enabling direct payments
recipients to access mainstream social and
educational facilities as an alternative to
day care. Such a strategy demands that
there is sufficient flexibility in funding for
day care and that this is not tied up
completely in block-purchased day care.

12

Independent Living

Choice and control

A great deal has been written from the perspective of younger disabled people about Independent Living. We know rather less about how older people define Independent Living and so this was one of our core questions. Our older participants' definitions of Independent Living were similar to those of younger disabled people in that they stressed issues of choice and control:

> **"Freedom of choice, when I say freedom, it's the freedom that you have, you choose who to have. You choose what the person should do. How to do it. How she should do it. When she should do it."**

> **"You got to control your own life rather than let other people run it for you."**

Independent Living was also defined as not having to continually ask social services or agencies to send care assistants who could fulfil their needs and requirements.

The Somali women also stressed control:

> **"Now I have more independence ... in control of my life. I can control everything but although I still have no energy ... but yes I can control everything."**

When we remarked to the Somali women that their definitions of independence were like those of our other older participants, they reminded us that "not everything is different".

For Mrs Young, it meant being "free of social services" and:

> **"I can do so much more, the sort of things I used to do before the stroke which makes me feel independent."**

Mrs Young felt that under direct services she was "cared for", which she equated partly with "being under the control of social services":

> **"They were making the decisions, they were deciding who came. Now it's me deciding."**

Mrs Young conceded that she might later want "more care, depending on the state of my health". She also felt that her impairment impinged upon her level of independence. She was not alone in this; Mrs Ungerson said she could not feel totally independent because she still needed "a lot of help". However, direct payments gave her "more independence" and, most importantly:

"It makes me feel I have an identity apart from my husband."

For Miss Dixon it was not always having to rely on her sister and

"Not being housebound, being able to get out when I want to, and being able to do what I want, when I want, and how I want."

For some older people, Independent Living was about getting the help they needed so that

"... you can get on with your ordinary life."

For Mrs Ward, Independent Living was about the "new lease of life" being on direct payments had given her, while for Mrs Smith it was being able to ask for what she wants, and no longer minding having to do so. In this context she also talked about her love of shopping.

For our participants, there were clear links between Independent Living, quality of life issues – most particularly the 'happiness factor' – and direct payments.

Care or personal assistance?

Some of our older participants equated 'care' by social services with loss of control over their own lives. That aside, they were less critical of the concept of care than may be found in the writings of the Disabled People's Movement (for example, Morris, 1993). The vast majority of our older participants were more comfortable with the term 'carer' than they were with 'personal assistant'. The Somali women tended to switch between 'carer' and 'worker' and confirmed that the concepts of care and carer they used were the same.

The older people equated 'care' in the context of direct payments with 'care tasks', and their employees or agency assistants as people who did the work of care. There were unmistakably substantial elements of mutual 'caring about' for many when they talked about their relationships with PAs; indeed, for one person this 'caring about' underpinned their preference for the term 'carer' rather than PA. At the same time, the majority also clearly felt in control of their support arrangements. There did not appear to be any dissonance between their use of the terms 'care' and 'carer' and their definitions of Independent Living. Indeed, one might argue that choosing the concepts and terms one is most comfortable with is a part of Independent Living.

13

The care managers' perspectives

In the absence of widespread information about and awareness of direct payments, care managers are key to informing older people about, and offering them access to, direct payments. Their attitudes towards, and confidence and willingness to consider, direct payments as an option for their clients are therefore crucial.

Care managers' perceptions of the advantages of direct payments

Advantages for older people

Most of the care managers we interviewed were emphatic that direct payments give more independence, control and flexibility to users than do direct services.

For some care managers, the issue of control was paramount. This, they felt, would give older people more of "a voice" and

"I just feel keeping people more in control gives them a better quality of life."

Independence was also stressed, including more independence *from* care managers, as older people were better able to 'care manage' themselves. Independence from the routines of care agencies was also recognised as an advantage to those older people who didn't want their lives controlled by these routines.

Some also recognised that greater control and independence could prevent or delay the need for residential care, as older people would feel better able to manage. Key to this was that informal carers managed both the direct payments and the support arrangements in situations where dementia-type conditions would otherwise make this unfeasible.

Advantages for care managers and local authorities

Time

Many, though not all, care managers pointed out that, once a direct payment package was in place, there was a positive impact upon their own workload. They no longer had to deal with "time consuming", "day-to-day care issues" such as care assistants not turning up or clients being unhappy with their providers. In contrast, as Marie said, "you don't need to put in very much input at all" with clients on direct payments.

Some care managers found setting up direct payments packages initially more time consuming but also felt that this was compensated for once the package was in place:

> **"When it works well, yes I'd say it's much less."**

A few care managers, however, believed that clients who were "a bit wobbly" in managing direct payments may "keep coming back" and that dealing with these clients could in itself be time consuming.

Job satisfaction

Some care managers were very enthusiastic about working with direct payments, stating this gave them a great deal of job satisfaction.

> **"It's so exciting!"**

> **"There's a massive sense of satisfaction."**

Clients, they said, were "empowered" by "actually being able to do it for themselves". Sometimes, they told us, by the time older people reached social services "things were looking awful" and they could feel they were losing control over their lives, but direct payments meant they could "take control of this area of their lives".

Problem solving

Many care managers used direct payments as a solution to particular problems, such as breakdowns in relationships between clients and providers, or where it had proved impossible to match clients with providers. One care manager told us direct payments "got us out of a hole". Her client "had been through all the agencies" and each time the relationship failed. Direct payments were the "last resort", but by giving the client "some amount of power to purchase her own care ... it's actually stabilised the thing" and "it has made it easier for us".

Direct payments also enabled clients to receive support in rural and other areas where there was a paucity of agency or in-house provision. One care manager regularly used direct payments in this situation to avoid having to use residential care until agency support could be organised, which, she said, could take weeks and be distressing for the older person.

Many of the older people living in rural areas had been there for many years and had social networks from which to find PAs, but some found it difficult. The care manager therefore collected names of potential PAs for her clients, for example, people already working as PAs, agency employees who wanted "to go independent" or "word of mouth around the office". She could not "recommend" anyone to her clients but she could give them her list and "suggest" people who might be available.

Increasing the take-up of direct payments

Care managers identified major barriers to increasing the take-up of direct payments by older people, the primary one being "the nature of the client group".

Care managers and their team managers explained that they "have a lot of people with dementia" who "wouldn't be suitable" for direct payments unless there was an informal carer who could manage the scheme on their behalf.

The legality of giving direct payments to informal carers of a person who does not have the capacity to consent and who even with assistance would not be able to manage the money is questionable. However, a recent judgement by the High Court held that it was lawful to give the payments to a User Independent Trust to arrange services for an individual in this situation (see Schwer, 2003).

We did not come across any examples of such trusts in the research. We did, however, find varying practices within local authorities, with some teams offering direct payments for informal carers to manage and other areas which saw this as contrary to policy and practice guidance.

Many care managers also felt that tightening the eligibility criteria meant that those receiving help were "really quite poorly", rendering direct payments an unfeasible option. Here the majority of care managers tended not to offer direct payments to older people they considered "frail", living alone and without a network of support. However, as some concurred, this probably indicated a "protective attitude" towards older people.

In contrast, care managers in one team used an arguably more enabling criterion: they offered direct payments to any client who could talk about their needs and understand the assessment process without requiring the assistance of a third party (although one might be present).

These care managers, like others, said that most older people refused direct payments. They preferred to have the care manager organise the support because they didn't want to have to find their own workers or deal with the administrative demands. But it was important that care managers did not presume this and make generalisations which then stereotype and discriminate against older people.

The care managers who had been most successful in promoting direct payments to older people stressed that the way they presented this option was all-important:

> **"... if you go, 'oh you could have direct payments I suppose, but then you'd have to write the contracts and ugh' nobody's going to say 'gosh that sounds good'. But if you say 'we've got direct payments and that would free you up to employ someone, it could happen when you want, it's based on our assessment of your needs but you can be much more flexible' then people might think 'we'll try that'."**

Peter stressed that it was important that care managers are themselves enthusiastic about direct payments:

> **"I believe you've got to actually believe in it yourself, be positive about it. There is a lot**

of paperwork but I think if you go into it 'hey, here's an alternative'."

Essential prerequisites are that care managers have sufficient knowledge themselves about direct payments, the support of their immediate line managers, time to think, and a clear understanding of what direct payments support services can offer.

Care managers' knowledge of direct payments

The less care managers understand about direct payments , the more unlikely they are to offer them:

> **"I just don't understand it. It's not user-friendly. And because I don't understand it, I don't think I can explain it."**

It is, then, important to look at how to increase care managers' knowledge base and hence confidence in offering direct payments.

Contact and joint visits to clients with support service workers could build up care managers' confidence, experience and knowledge. Debbie told us that getting help from the Borough's direct payments support service with setting up her client on direct payments had been "a learning process". She particularly appreciated that there was "an open door" and that she could ask any question "no matter how silly".

Other care managers made similar points, while many said that inviting direct-payments support service workers to team meetings had been, or would be,

helpful. They would "hear the same song from the same singer" instead of going to training in twos or threes and hearing slightly different versions.

Attending training days on direct payments was also seen as important in building up knowledge and confidence. Sometimes this was difficult, particularly for part-time staff and where the training took place away from the work base. Locally based rather than centrally based training would, therefore, be useful.

Overall it appeared that those care managers who were most knowledgeable and confident were also those who had had input from the direct payments support service, had worked with direct payments, and had been able to attend training events on direct payments.

Importance of contact with direct payments support services

As has been indicated, care managers gained a lot of knowledge and confidence from their contact with direct payments support service workers. It also became apparent that they needed to understand the level and type of support that was available to their clients from these services if they were to be able to implement the 'willing and able' criteria attached to direct payments.

Before setting up a direct payments package, care managers need to ensure that the individual has consented and is able to manage direct payments alone or with support. In the City, implementing the 'willing and able' criteria was in fact within the remit of the direct payments support service, but even here care managers needed to exercise some level of professional judgement when deciding to whom to introduce direct payments before referring them to the support service.

Not all the care managers we met were totally au fait with the 'willing and able' criteria, though in discussion it did appear they were using their professional judgement, even if some called it a "gut feeling".

While some care managers in the Borough and the County immediately referred older people who showed interest in direct payments to the support service, others waited until their client had reached a decision. The timing is important: support service workers suggested that early referrals tend to have a more positive outcome with regard to uptake.

Some care managers were uncertain about the remit of the support services, and wanted more information so that they could "emphasise the support available" when offering direct payments.

There were, however, sometimes tensions between care management teams and support services in that some team managers clearly felt that support service workers "promised" clients more than local authorities could afford. They also feared that support service workers might "mislead" care managers by implying that direct payments users could get more hours than other service users.

Some care managers also wished that support service workers wouldn't "promise the earth", leaving care managers looking "like grim reapers" because they had to work within budgetary constraints. Nevertheless, care managers also understood that getting the best deal for their clients was within the remit of the support service:

"We're coming from two different places and I think because they work with disabled people all the time they are carrying the flag for them."

In practice, it seemed that there was mutual respect and understanding between the two groups, which facilitated their working together. However, some team managers remained concerned to ensure equity between direct payment users and direct service users, and were 'suspicious' of the aspirations of support services.

The City system did not easily lend itself to joint working between support service workers and care managers. Here, care managers handed over their assessments to the support service to follow up. They then saw their role as completed (unless the referral was returned because the older person was deemed either unwilling or unable), to the extent that some believed that support service workers were also responsible for reviews of the care plan.

Importance of relationship with front–line managers

Those care managers most confident and successful in giving older people access to direct payments stressed how important it was to have supportive team managers who empowered them to translate policy into practice. They pointed out that setting up a direct payments package could be "loads of work":

"It's not slap in a package, wait for 28 days, review it and that's it. It's not like that."

It was then essential to "have a team manager who's supportive and encouraging" because "you need to have the space and the permission to spend time on one person":

"You've got to feel you've got time before you *can* think. You need to feel the comfort of the time in order to think 'how can I do this?' You have to have the feeling of time to do it before you can think of doing it. She makes me feel that I've got the space to think."

The importance of this was evident in some other teams in which care managers felt controlled rather than supported by their team managers.

A small minority of the care managers told us that they felt "totally deskilled". Their care plans were scrutinised by their team manager to the extent that they felt their professionalism was being questioned. New referrals were not prioritised but "just thrown at" them, and "you're under pressure to go out whether or not it's a real priority". The pressure they felt under is exemplified in the following statements:

"You're in, assess, you put the service in, get out and get onto the next person. Half the time I don't even think about direct payments because I haven't got the time."

"You just haven't got time to think creatively."

Putting an interim care package in place while the older person considered direct payments was dismissed as "doubling the work".

Care managers who were in the more fortunate position of feeling supported by their team managers also told us how important it was to be enabled to deal with their initial anxieties in working with direct payments:

"You need to feel enabled, if you're anxious about it you need someone to encourage you."

"You've got to have confidence to do this and [team manager] gives you the confidence, so to me she is part of it."

Time constraints

Time was a major issue for many care managers: their high caseloads and what they felt was overwhelming bureaucratisation of the job meant a difficult balancing act between face-to-face client work on the one hand, and computer work and meeting the increasing demand for statistics on the other. Some said they struggled "to keep all the balls in the air" and that the impact of this could be that care managers "get stuck in a rut" and then:

"… it's so easy to stay with the same old things, same old stuff."

Staying with the "same old stuff" meant in effect heading "straight into mainstream services", and as Helen said:

"I think that's the culture to be honest, to go straight into mainstream."

The combination of time and work pressures on care managers in older people's teams can stifle innovative and imaginative work that looks beyond physical maintenance to quality of life issues (Gorman and Postle, 2003). As one team manager said:

"If you've got a waiting list of people who are really at risk to life and limb needing care packages put in, you're hardly going to think about the social stuff. It's what's essential work and what's desirable work on the part of care managers, isn't it."

It is, however, possible to challenge this imposed dichotomy. When we asked Helen why she broke out of the rut, she replied simply:

"Because I see happier people."

Translating community care assessments into flexible direct payments packages

A key to the success of direct payments lies in translating a community care assessment into a direct payments package without removing the flexibility which allows people to take control. As Hasler et al (1998) say, the care plan which describes the individual's needs and aims and which forms the basis of the hours allocated each week can be used as a template. But it misses the point of direct payments if this is then used to dictate the individual's routine and how they can use their direct payments.

All of the care managers interviewed agreed that direct payments should enable the recipient to determine their own daily routines. There were, however, differences between care managers over the second area of flexibility: what direct payments could be used for.

Most care managers held that there had to be accountability for how direct payments were used because this was "public money". At the same time, they had "to be aware" of their local authority's "budgetary demands" when deciding the hours to be allocated a direct payments package, work to their local authority's eligibility criteria and adhere to what was considered an eligible need. This last amounted in effect to the need for assistance with personal care.

Some care managers and their line managers held that direct payments should be used only to meet eligible or essential needs and not desirable needs for which the local authority did not otherwise provide. Gardening and going on holiday were frequently mentioned in this context. Such use, they said, was "abuse" of direct payments and also created inequities between directly provided services users and direct payments users.

A small number of care managers extended this to what in-house and agency home-care services could and could not provide – what service resources were available to older people. Some said it would be impossible, for example, for home care to provide a care assistant to accompany an older person on an outing. In discussion, however, most of these care managers agreed that the focus of their criticism should be on inflexible service resources rather than upon flexible use of direct payments.

Perceptions like those outlined above were not in fact in line with the local authorities' stated policies. For example, the Borough's Policy and Procedure document stated that funding for other than "essential" needs was subject to availability of resources within the department, but:

"As a user of direct payments gains in experience they may also be able to use creativity and flexibility in the way in which their allocation is used in order to enhance their quality of life."

According to one senior manager, placing rigid restrictions upon the use of direct payments to meet only essential needs was probably due to the inexperience of direct payments among older persons' care management teams. They simply did not understand that Independent Living means more than personal care. The senior manager also confirmed that occasionally direct payments packages could legitimately be bigger and therefore more costly. This was because the need to pare down to precise time units for each activity was removed. In addition, packages need not be restricted to what direct services could provide. However, these 'permissions' seemed not to have filtered down to the care management teams.

Some care managers were more flexible than others in terms of what they accepted as an eligible need, even if they were not always able to specify this on the care plan. 'Subterfuge' to get the best

for clients was not unheard of among these care managers, even if it did lead to inequities. As one said:

"I don't care if I can get more for one than can I manage for another. That doesn't give me a problem because I'm always trying to do my best for that one at that time."

Few care managers believed that they should 'police' the way their older clients were using direct payments, but some were more confident than others in letting their clients get on with it. They recognised that personal care need not be restricted to one location – the home – and that personal assistance could be employed by clients to do "some of the things [they] enjoy" so long as the care plan held a "core of personal care" because "personal care opens the door". One care manager summed up the necessity of allowing clients to get on with it:

"Direct payments are meant to be about taking control of your life. But if we place restrictions on them, they're not in control, are they. We are."

Nevertheless, even the most 'liberal' of care managers were restricted by budgets when allocating hours to a direct payments package. Within this context we were repeatedly told that care packages in general were smaller for older people than they were for other adult user groups and that service resources, particularly for social activities, were more restricted.

Inequity between younger and older people

It was difficult to identify the precise mechanisms underpinning inequities between younger and older people. In one of the local authorities lower cost ceilings were applied to packages for older people than for other adult user groups. Lower cost ceilings have historically curtailed the development and use of innovative care packages and have demonstrated the lower priority accorded to older people's independence (Henwood, 2002). This has undoubtedly affected the culture of social work/care management with older people and continues to do so even where differential cost ceilings no longer apply.

The perception of many care managers and their team managers was that eligibility criteria were more rigidly interpreted for older people than for younger adults, and that some needs regarded as 'essential' for younger adults were downgraded to 'desirable' for older people.

Some felt that inequities might have been the product of the greater voice of younger disabled people who were "more articulate about their needs", and, crucially, the greater willingness of social services to listen to them.

Others, however, believed that younger disabled people often had wider and more complex needs than older people, necessitating bigger care or direct payments packages. This perception may reflect the low priority and merit accorded to older people's needs beyond those concerned with minimal physical maintenance, and disregards the social,

emotional and psychological factors that make life worth living.

Changing the culture of care management

With few exceptions, direct payments have a long way to go before they could be described as part of the culture of older persons' care management teams. Care managers and their immediate line managers readily admitted this, but also voiced their commitment to changing the culture.

Pressures of work, together with 'the nature of the client group', were given as the primary reasons why most teams had relatively few older people on direct payments. But it was also the case that care managers' mind-sets were often geared more towards "going straight into mainstream services", which was seen as much easier than going down the route of direct payments. It seemed that, unless direct payments were requested, or there were specific problems that might be solved by direct payments, then they were not in the forefront of the minds of many care managers:

"I must admit, I haven't perhaps looked at it maybe as carefully as I should as an option when assessing people."

"I don't always think about it straight off."

"Direct payments don't go 'ping' in our heads."

Concerns were voiced by care managers reflecting a combination of 'paternalism' and a lack of certainty about particular aspects of direct payments. For example, one care manager worried about who undertook a risk assessment in relation to the care to be provided and who would be deemed responsible if the older person or the PA was injured in the course of the care. This care manager realised that direct payments users have specific responsibilities as employers and that they should have employers' liability insurance, but was unclear about the details:

"It worries me in one way, in that while everything's ticking over it's nobody's problem. But what if something goes wrong?"

A concern that older people would not be able to find employees and a reluctance to become involved in this issue constrained some care managers from offering direct payments. Additionally, some worried about the suitability of PAs and whether they would "do the job properly". One care manager felt that many older people would be "frightened" about letting strangers in and were happier with agency care assistants because they believed (if erroneously) that they had been police-checked. Others felt older people would simply be too nervous to employ people themselves and deal with the administrative tasks.

Care managers expressing such concerns were likely to say that they would offer direct payments only if there was an informal carer to manage them on the older person's behalf. In fact, with few exceptions, 'there needs to be an informal carer' was almost a mantra of care managers.

It will take time to change the culture of older people's care management teams so as to embrace direct payments. The

commitment is there, but needs to be matched by a realisation that with the right support direct payments can work, and work well, for older people. Most importantly, care managers and their team managers need to be proactive in listening to the views, experiences and perceptions of older people who are successfully working with direct payments.

14

The importance of support services in making direct payments work for older people

The importance of established direct-payments support services in making direct payments schemes work for disabled people has been widely recognised (Hasler et al, 1999; DoH, 2003c). The situation is no different for older people. However, older people are among the new direct payments user groups; and it was the perception of many of the support service workers who participated in this research that new user groups often needed more intensive forms of support.

Help with recruitment

Recruiting PAs was said by one support service coordinator to be the biggest issue facing people receiving direct payments.

Many older people appreciated, or would have appreciated, access to a PA register held by the direct payments support services. Finding PAs was not easy, and registers were also seen as a relatively safe means of recruitment.

Only the Borough's support service maintained such a register. However, keeping this updated was costly and time-consuming and required the assistance of

a working group. This, together with sufficient flexibility in its funding from the local authority, enabled the service to respond to this user demand.

A further initiative on the part of the Borough's support service was to raise the profile of PA work in its promotion events in order to attract more people to the job. This involved including details about PA work in displays, giving out PA packs, and running a PA open forum event. Consultation with existing PAs also threw up ideas for "very basic" training and induction, covering disability awareness and what the job might entail.

The County's support service had maintained a PA register in the past with funding from the County. However, the nature of the County – its mix of rural, urban and coastal areas over a wide geographical area – made it inefficient to maintain at that time. This is an issue that the County is currently reconsidering. In the City, attention was being paid to this issue but, as an in-house service, it led to uncertainties about the local authority's legal position vis-à-vis PAs on such a register.

Other areas of help related to the recruitment process included help with the wording of advertisements, advice and assistance with interviewing and help drawing up contracts of employment. These forms of help were available in all three of our areas and were highly valued by those of our participants who used them.

Managing the financial and other administrative tasks associated with direct payments

Support service workers and older people identified support in managing the finances and administration as crucial to making direct payments work for older people. In fact, some support workers felt that these were the areas that most worried older people.

Probably the most comprehensive support here was available in the City, where the in-house support service offered a payroll and audit service and an external accountancy service.

The Borough's support service was able to pay the costs of any payroll service the individual chose through top-up monies. The support service workers otherwise provided the necessary advice and support as and when needed.

As will be further outlined, the service specification between the County and its support scheme prioritised new direct payments users who were in the first six months of using the scheme. However, it was clear that many older people required ongoing support with their quarterly returns. Getting that support was invaluable to them:

"It's just like a weight lifted. It would worry me. I've never

kept books, I never kept accounts … I'm just weary. All I want to do is just flop in the chair."

An accessible and personalised service

A number of older people told us how important it was to access support services easily on the phone, particularly "if you are having difficulty". Many people said that it was crucial to operate a telephone duty system during office hours so that there was always someone available. As one woman said, it was "frightening when you're on your own and you've got no one to turn to".

Some older people described the support service workers as "like family" offering security and "caring". Others pointed out that it was usually easier to get hold of support workers than care managers.

People who had crossed the SSD administrative boundary between 'adult' and 'older persons' services sometimes had particular needs for support. This could be because they feared their hours would be reduced or because they had lost their known care manager and now had to rely upon a duty team, leaving them with "no backup" within social services. One older person stressed how important it was that support service workers fully understand these concerns and adjust their communication styles to reassure people in this situation. She also pointed to the need for support service workers to get to know their older clients by listening and talking to them more and thus be able to offer a personalised service.

Information

Getting information that was timely and accurate was important to the older participants.

Newsletters and information sheets were found to be informative and helpful, although some felt a bit overwhelmed by the number of information sheets sent out, and one suggested that support services provide a ready-made filing system to help clients keep the papers in order.

Some older participants found the information packs that are initially sent out to potential direct payments users a bit cumbersome:

> **"It could have been helpful if I'd have read it properly, but you don't. You read it in bits and pieces. There's too much of it, I think."**

Many felt the packs would be better "scaled down a bit".

Getting clear information, understanding and encouragement from support service workers was very important for both deciding whether to accept direct payments and how to manage them. Miss Turner, for example, said that when she first received "all the jargon" she thought she "would never manage this". Things were getting "so bad" with her directly provided services she was "thinking of going into a home". However, the support service coordinator was "so kind and understanding" that Miss Turner realised that "with a bit of gumption" and support she "could do it".

The experience of one of our older participants shows by default how important information and support is. Mr Cox managed his neighbour's direct payment because there was "nobody else to do it" and the only alternative was nursing home care. Mr Cox did not know he would have to make returns every quarter when he first took it on, or that he would face a "mountain of paperwork". One of the problems, he said, was that "you don't know what you don't know" and therefore it's difficult to ask the right questions:

> **"... it's an uphill struggle to get it done because there's always the time and problems. And nobody ever tells you the wrinkles, and how to get round the wrinkles."**

The only support he received was from his neighbour's care manager; he was unaware of the existence of the support service. This was the case with some others in the County – some care managers had simply not followed the procedures for putting direct payments users in touch with the support service.

Training for older direct payments users

Most of the training for older people on direct payments appeared to take place on a one-to-one basis. This could be very time consuming, and in the Borough the support service had started to run training sessions for small groups at a local resource centre for disabled people. The support service coordinator felt that it was a good use of her time as well as inspiring participants to "feed off each other" and "ask more questions".

The City support service used to provide group training on a one-off basis but this did not prove as effective as ongoing one-to-one input from support service workers and the audit officer.

None of our older participants reported receiving training in being an employer, although the Personal Assistance User Group in the Borough fulfilled much of that function. Our older participants did, however, receive information from support services on their responsibilities as employers. Yet, as already noted, some were unsure about their responsibility vis-à-vis employers' liability insurance and notifying the Inland Revenue.

Peer support and the involvement of older people

All three areas provided opportunities for peer support groups, usually through the direct payments support service but sometimes through other user organisations. The Borough's support service seemed most successful: some older people regularly attended the local Personal Assistant User Group meetings and were represented on the management committee. The County and the City support services, by contrast, generally found it difficult to attract direct payments users to meetings and policy advisory groups.

It is impossible to say why these differences exist. There also remains the question of what is meant by 'peer' support. Does the term 'peer' refer to the common experience of disability? And how does this coalesce with experience of ageing? Do the concerns of younger disabled people necessarily reflect those

of older people and vice versa? How does peer support work in ethnically mixed groups? Such questions are worthy of further research.

In this research project, only a few older people described themselves as involved in user groups. Some said it was simply too difficult to attend meetings, either because their PAs were not available to accompany them or because they found it physically uncomfortable to sit in the provided seating for any length of time. Others said it simply wasn't their thing and for a small number this seemed to be about not identifying with younger disabled adults and sometimes finding the groups "too political".

However, those who did attend meetings found them useful

"... because you find out what's going on, so you do get more of a rounded picture."

Recognising that there might be specific issues excluding older people from meetings, the Borough's support service was considering different ways of enabling their participation, including facilitating small peer-support groups of older people meeting in their own homes.

15

Funding of support services

Support services require funding by local authorities to a level commensurate with making direct payments schemes a success, to increase capacity and to make their service appropriate to the needs of the diverse communities they serve.

A Policy Studies Institute (PSI) study recommended that one support worker could support 30 users when schemes are developed (Hasler et al, 1998). A higher ratio of users to workers could, the study said, undermine the quality of support provided, but there are no government guidelines on this, and so there can be wide variation between local authority areas. This was the certainly the case with the areas participating in this research project.

In the Borough, the local authority funded three full-time staff posts to serve 80 direct payments users. The local authority usually funded a staff to client ratio of 1.5:50, but at the time of the research funding was increased for promotional and development work with under-represented groups.

The City's in-house support service was not subject to a separate funding agreement. There were three Independent Living advisers, a payroll officer and an audit officer serving 155 clients. Both the City and the Borough provided ongoing support to existing and new direct payments users.

In the County, the support service's staff to client ratio was 2.8:600. An additional 0.5 post was funded from the mental health budget to pilot direct payments with people experiencing mental health difficulties, while two 0.5 posts were funded through another organisation to provide support for informal carers receiving direct payments in their own right.

The County's contract with the support service specified that priority should be given to people in the first six months of receiving direct payments, with lower priority for longer-term users. People with longer-term support needs had the responsibility along with their care managers to consider such issues before signing the letter of agreement. The support service reported to us that in one typical quarter it had dealt with 119 people, 59 of whom were new to, or were considering, direct payments.

Not only might older people require more ongoing support, as was shown by this research, but working with new recipients can be time-intensive. Furthermore, support service workers in the County cover a wide geographical area, adding to time and travel costs.

These factors must be seen as impacting upon the level of service that can be provided. As one support worker said, "we don't have a lot of time for development work".

Despite the difficulties faced by the support service in the County, many of our older County participants praised it and its workers, some evaluating it as "excellent".

Local authorities may regard meeting the PSI recommendations as reducing the cost-effectiveness of direct payments to untenable levels in terms of achieving best value. However, it should be remembered that the quality of a direct payments scheme is dependent to a large extent upon quality support. The Direct Payments Development Fund may lead to new initiatives that achieve best value. But central government needs to provide longer-term ring-fenced funding if its policy objective of making direct payments a reality for "tens of thousands of older people" (DoH, 2003a) is to be realised.

Value of direct payments support services to local authorities

Local authorities derive value from direct payments support services above and beyond ensuring best value for direct payment users, which was, however, paramount.

Support services can take the strain off local authorities by releasing care management time for working with clients who required substantial care manager input. This was particularly the case in the City, where the support services implemented the 'willing and able' criteria, but was also evident in the County and the Borough, depending on the point at which care managers brought in the support service. Clearly, both areas could have benefited even more if all care managers referred people to the support service for assistance in deciding whether or not to take up direct payments. More generally, support services remove the necessity for care managers to deal with the day-to-day issues arising from service delivery. As a senior manager told us, support services are able to spend more time with clients than care managers are, and there is no need for care managers to become involved in recruitment and employment issues.

Support services are also useful to local authorities in terms of the training and information functions for care management teams. The importance of these functions has already been outlined, but it is worth reiterating the central importance of care managers and support services in introducing older people's access to direct payments.

As indicated, the paramount value of support services is that they enable older people to successfully work with direct payments. One senior manager told us that while local authorities had to consider cost-effectiveness, this had to incorporate the value to the client of increased flexibility and greater independence. Funding direct payments support services to make this possible and to take the strain off care managers was perceived as value for money. The view of the senior manager was that:

"It pays dividends."

Independent or in-house support services?

In the City our older participants were unperturbed by the fact that the social services department provided their support service. They were more concerned about the qualities of the people providing the support and the quality of that support. In fact, they were all happy with both.

Some older people in the Borough appreciated the distance created between them and the social services department by the role of the support service in making and monitoring the payments. They wanted to have as little as possible to do with social services. In the County, some older participants expressed their appreciation of independent support, and while few were politically active, they were also encouraged by the support service's ability to campaign on issues that affected them.

Workers from the independent support services and senior managers from the relevant local authorities stressed the importance of user-led organisations providing the support function. As one senior manager said, independent organisations could challenge local authorities, remind them sometimes of their responsibilities, and ensure that not all the control was held within one agency "with all its constraints". Another stated that user-led organisations better enabled partnership and consultation between users and the local authority, and were essential to adhering to the philosophy of Independent Living and to partnership and consultation.

Conclusions

16

This report has shown that direct payments can improve older people's quality of life. Crucially, older people receiving direct payments reported feeling happier than they had been, or would have been, receiving directly provided services. They were more relaxed, more motivated, and able to do more. Creating and managing their support arrangements to meet their own preferences made them feel more independent, and had a positive impact upon their social, emotional and physical health. Having control over their support arrangements enabled some older people to avoid residential care.

Direct payments also enabled Somali older participants to secure services that met their language and cultural requirements. While it would be unwise to generalise the Somali experience to other Black and minority ethnic groups, the ways in which the barriers to their getting access to and managing direct payments were overcome may provide transferable lessons. These included the use of an accountancy service to deal with the banking, audit and administrative demands, and the forging of a direct link between community outreach workers and the direct-payments support service.

Direct payments are not well-known among older people, and so increasing their uptake means devising different ways of getting information to them. Care managers are an important source of information but older people also suggest using national and local radio, and posting information in health, housing, community and social settings. Direct payments support services also have a promotional role and might consider how they can develop links with under-represented groups within the community.

The majority of our older participants used their direct payments to employ PAs. They successfully adapted transferable skills from past career and life experiences. A range of methods was used to recruit PAs, but recruitment was not easy, and there was a call for direct payments support services to maintain registers of potential PAs.

Some older people used their PAs to enable them to enjoy social and leisure activities outside the home and/or to develop alternatives to residential respite care. Such usage is in accord with the ethos of Independent Living underpinning the direct payments legislation. However, older people were rarely accorded hours for this within their direct payments packages, and so had to make creative use of their payments and subsidise them to meet the extra costs.

There was a widespread perception among all our participants that the social and leisure needs of older people are not deemed as essential or as eligible as they are for other adult user groups. Most direct payments packages for older people were based primarily upon personal care needs, reflecting an ethos embedded in statutory provision that older people have a more restricted lifestyle than younger adults. This is underscored by a history of lower cost ceilings, less innovative commissioning practices and the fragmentation of services and resources for disabled and older people.

Fair Access to Care Services (FACS) should address these inequities and encourage a conceptualisation of independence which recognises involvement and social participation. However, fundamental discriminatory attitudes may be more difficult to displace. At the same time it is difficult to see how FACS will address the detrimental impact of the work pressures experienced by care management teams upon their capacity to work in more creative ways with older people. That involves taking on board the social, emotional and psychological factors that make life worth living.

The government's policy objective of rooting out age discrimination is contradicted by the exclusion of older people from applying to the Independent Living 93 Fund. This both neglects the increased costs incurred by the combination of impairment and ageing, and contributes to the inequity of lower cost ceilings.

The government is also determined to remove the 'Berlin Wall' between health and social care, but there was little evidence of success in this. Older people found it absurd that they could not purchase professional services like chiropody and physiotherapy with their direct payments. There were no instances where health authorities had contributed to a direct payments package, and so older people used their PAs to meet some of these needs. This was not always possible, however. Wider use of the flexibilities of the 1999 Health Act could enable older people to meet needs that are essential to the maintenance of their health and mobility and therefore to their independence and social participation.

Local authority care managers have a crucial role to play in extending direct payments to older people. This requires a change in the culture of care management to embrace direct payments as a positive option.

Care managers expressed their commitment to cultural change. To achieve this, they need knowledge and confidence, the leadership and support of their immediate line managers, time to think and work creatively, and a clear understanding of the role of direct payments support services. They also need to consider *how* they present direct payments as an option to their older clients. Stressing that direct payments offer benefits and flexibility and that support is available is more likely to yield positive results than transferring concerns to their clients about older people's ability to manage direct payments.

Care managers' confidence in working with direct payments can be enhanced by working in partnership with support services. Care managers also need to appreciate the clear benefits of direct payments to their clients and to themselves. Those care managers who had successfully worked with direct payments stressed the resultant job satisfaction they experienced from seeing happier people who are in control of their lives.

A key to the success of direct payments lies in ensuring that the translation of a community care plan into a direct payments package does not remove the flexibility of allowing individuals to take control (Hasler et al, 1999). While few care managers felt that they should police the way their clients were using direct payments, they faced tensions created by budgetary constraints and eligibility criteria in allocating sufficient hours to direct payments packages to meet needs beyond those of personal care. The tensions were compounded for some by concerns about maintaining equity between direct payments users and directly provided service users. Care managers need clear understanding that Independent Living means more than personal care; however, that understanding must be backed up by clear policy statements from senior management about the scope and permitted uses of direct payment packages.

There was little awareness among care management teams of the scope of the 2000 Carers and Disabled Children Act, and there were no instances in which informal carers had been offered direct payments in their own right. Furthermore, the sorts of needs which informal carers had – usually for domestic help – were deemed not to meet eligibility criteria.

Direct payments support services played a crucial role in enabling many of our older participants to enjoy direct payments. Some older people required the early support and encouragement of support service workers in reaching the decision that they could manage direct payments. The administrative and audit demands were the major difficulty faced by older people and many would have found these demands too great without ongoing assistance from support services. Specific forms of impairment and sheer exhaustion added to the difficulties some older participants experienced in managing these demands. Local authorities need to consider whether their procedures for accountability are user-friendly. They also need to ensure that appropriate support is in place and that this is adequately financed.

Direct payments support services require funding to a level commensurate with meeting the needs of a widening client group of direct payments recipients. Funding must enable support services to adapt to the needs of different client groups, and to promote direct payments among under-represented groups. Adequate funding of support services can achieve best value by ensuring a quality service. Cost effectiveness may be an issue for local authorities as increasing numbers of direct payments packages demand expanded support services. On the one hand, consultation and strategic planning in partnership with support services are required. On the other, while the Direct Payments Development Fund may address some of the shortfalls and lead to innovative ways of supporting older people receiving direct payments, it is vital that this leads to sustainable and realistic levels of funding for support services. Central government's aspirations to expand direct payments may need to be matched by ring-fenced funding for support services.

Peer support is a key element of a direct payment support service. However, it is unclear what 'peer' means. The majority of older people benefited from and appreciated the expertise of direct payments support service workers, and many found support service workers approachable and helpful. However, few were involved in group and policy meetings, and for some this was because they did not identify with younger disabled people.

Direct payments support services may usefully consider ways to fulfil the peer support needs of older people. One proposed initiative was to facilitate small group meetings in older people's own homes. This would enable older people to support each other and feed into wider policy and practice development. Local authorities are also concerned to ensure consultation with older people but some struggle to find organised groups *of* older people as opposed to carers' groups and organisations *for* older people.

It is vital that older people have a voice in the further development of direct payments; and local authorities may need to consider, perhaps in partnership with support services, how to facilitate the development of older people's groups where these do not yet exist. However, there are currently over 1,000 older people receiving direct payments whose experience and expertise could be an invaluable resource to draw upon for the benefit of other older people considering and taking up direct payments.

References

Audit Commission (1997) *The coming of age: Improving care services for older people*, London: Audit Commission.

Barnes, C. (1997) *Older people's perceptions of direct payments and self operated support systems*, Leeds: British Council of Disabled People's (BCODP) Research Unit, University of Leeds.

Clark, H. and Spafford, J. (2001) *Piloting choice and control for older people: An evaluation*, Bristol/York: The Policy Press/Joseph Rowntree Foundation.

Clark, H. and Spafford, J. (2002) 'Adapting to the culture of user control?', *Social Work Education*, vol 21, no 2, pp 247-57.

Clark, H., Dyer, S. and Horwood, J. (1998) *'That bit of help': The high value of low level services for older people*, Bristol/York: The Policy Press/Joseph Rowntree Foundation.

Dawson, C. (2000) *Independent successes: Implementing direct payments*, York: York Publishing Services/Joseph Rowntree Foundation.

DoH (Department of Health) (1998) *Modernising social services*, London: The Stationery Office.

DoH (2000) *Community Care (Direct Payments) Act 1996 Policy and Practice Guidance* (revised), London: DoH.

DoH (2001a) *National service framework for older people*, London: DoH.

DoH (2001b) *Carers and Disabled Children Act 2000: Policy guidance*, London: DoH.

DoH (2002a) *Community Care (Direct Payments) Act 1996: Draft consultation policy and practice guidance to direct payments*, London: DoH.

DoH (2002b) *Fair access to care services, policy guidance* (LAC (2002)13), London: DoH.

DoH (2002c) *Social services performance assessment framework indicators 2001-2002*, London: Government Statistical Service and DoH.

DoH (2003a) DoH website: www.doh.gov.uk/directpayments/index.htm (accessed 24 February 2003).

DoH (2003b) *Community care statistics 2001-2002: Referrals, assessments and packages of care for adults (England)*, London: DoH.

DoH (2003c) *Direct Payments Guidance Community Care: Services for Carers and Children's Services (Direct Payments) Guidance (England)*, London: DoH.

DoH/SSI (Social Services Inspectorate) (1998) *They look after their own, don't they?: The report of the national inspection of community care services for black and ethnic minority older people*, London: DoH.

DoH/SSI (2000) *New directions for Independent Living*, London: DoH Publications.

DIG (Disablement Income Group) (1996) *Personal assistance support schemes and the introduction of direct payments: Report and recommendations*, London: DIG.

George, M. (2003) 'Calculating the cost', *Care and Health*, no 32, pp 16-18.

Glasby, J. and Littlechild, R. (2002) *Social work and direct payments*, Bristol: The Policy Press.

Glendinning, C., Halliwell, S., Jacobs, S., Rummery, K., and Tyer, J. (2000) *Buying independence*, Bristol/York: The Policy Press/Joseph Rowntree Foundation.

Gorman, H. and Postle, K. (2003) *Transforming community care: A distorted vision?*, Birmingham: Venture Press.

Harding, T. (1997) *A life worth living: The independence and inclusion of older people*, London: Help the Aged.

Hasler, F., Campbell, J. and Zarb, G. (1999) *Direct routes to independence: A guide to local authority implementation and management of direct payments*, London: Policy Studies Institute.

Hasler, F., Zarb, G. and Campbell, J. (1998) *Key issues for local authority implementation of direct payments*, London: Policy Studies Institute.

Henwood, M. (2002) 'Age discrimination in social care', in Help the Aged, *Age discrimination in public policy: A review of evidence*, London: Help the Aged.

HM Customs and Excise (2003) Business Brief, 1 March, www.hmce.gov.uk/news/bb-013.htm

Kestenbaum, A. (1995) *An opportunity lost? Social services use of the independent living transfer*, London: the DIG.

Milburn, A. (2002) 'Reforming social services', speech to the 2002 Annual Social Services Conference, Cardiff, 16 October.

Morris, J. (1993) *Independent lives? Community care and disabled* people, Basingstoke: Macmillan.

NCIL (National Centre for Independent Living) (2002) *NCIL response to Community Care (Direct Payments) Act 1996. Draft policy and practice guidance consultation paper*, www.ncil.org.uk/dpconsult_response02.asp (accessed 21 February 2003).

Schwer, B. (2003) 'User independent trusts and the law', *Care and Health*, no 29 (12-25 February), pp 36-7.

SSI (Social Services Inspectorate) (1998) *That's the way the money goes*, London: DoH.

SSI (2000) *Modern social services: A commitment to people. The 9th annual report of the Chief Inspector of Social Services*, London: DoH.

SSI (2002) *Improving older people's services – Policy into practice. The second phase of inspections into older people's services*, London: DoH.

Vasey, S. (2000) *The rough guide to managing personal assistants*, London: NCIL.

Zarb, G. (1995) 'Direct payments legislation: prospects and pitfalls', in C. Glendinning, S. Halliwell, S. Jacobs, K. Rummery and J. Tyer, *Buying independence*, Bristol/York: The Policy Press/Joseph Rowntree Foundation.

Zarb, G. (1998) 'What price independence?', Keynote speech to the NCIL conference '*Shaping our futures*', London, www.ncil.org.uk

Zarb, G. and Nadash, P. (1994) *Cashing in on independence*, Clay Cross: BCODP.

Zarb, G. and Oliver, M. (1993) *Ageing with a disability: What do they expect after all these years?*, London: University of Greenwich.

Appendix: Methodology

Research methods

The research was undertaken between January 2002 and July 2003 in three English local authority areas: a London borough (the Borough), a southern county (the County) and a city council in the north-west (the City). Each area is geographically and demographically diverse, and has different mechanisms of making and supporting direct payments.

Having gained approval from the relevant local authorities or agencies, we adopted qualitative 'case study' research methods to determine 'what works' for older people using direct payments. In order to reflect the diversity of older people's experiences, older people on direct payments were invited to participate through a range of forums: a focus group, discussion group(s), and pair and individual interviews.

Forty-one older people from the three local authority areas who were in receipt of direct payments participated in the research, as did five senior managers, 32 care managers and 11 team managers, plus 10 direct payments support scheme workers. Data analysis was ongoing throughout the research process; a constant comparative analysis approach was adopted

The research process

Phase One

We used a focus group of older people in the London borough in order to gain some initial insights and understanding, and to inform the final research design. The focus group was reconvened on three other occasions to continue to act in a consultative capacity.

Contacts with local authorities, Centres for Independent Living, support schemes and other relevant agencies were consolidated.

Phase Two

Older people on direct payments living in the County and the Borough were invited to participate in the research process and then interviewed either individually or in pairs.

After receiving each older person's permission to do so, we contacted and interviewed those key personnel who were working with him or her. In addition, we interviewed care managers who were or had been successful in implementing direct payments with other older people.

Phase Three

Contact was established with the Somali community leaders and interpreters in the City, and as a result two discussion groups were held with six Somali older women.

The discussion groups were conducted with the help of an interpreter, and although using an interpreter is fraught with difficulties, we believe that we have been able to reflect accurately the experiences of the Somali women.

Other older recipients of direct payments living in the City were also interviewed, as were care managers, support scheme workers and key social services staff.

Phase Four

Following the completion of the draft report, final consultations were held with the focus group, the Centres for Independent Living, key local authority staff and other relevant agencies to ensure its accuracy and fairness and the mutual anonymity of the participants.

Also available from The Policy Press in association with the Joseph Rowntree Foundation

Piloting choice and control for older people
An evaluation
Heather Clark and Jan Spafford

This practical report is based on an evaluation of an innovative pilot scheme set up to find new ways to deliver services to older people, giving them greater choice and control. Based on interviews held with older users and care managers involved in the pilot scheme, it looks at older people's perceptions of this scheme and draws out broader lessons for service delivery.

Paperback £14.95 ($25.00) ISBN 1 86134 243 8

297 x 210mm 84 pages April 2001

'Put yourself in my place'
Designing and managing care homes for people with dementia
Caroline Cantley and Robert C. Wilson

'Put yourself in my place' is an excellent guide based to the latest thinking about person-centred dementia care. It draws upon case studies of recently built specialist dementia care homes to produce practical suggestions about designing, setting up and managing specialist care home facilities for people with dementia.

Paperback £16.95 (US$29.95) ISBN 1 86134 389 2

297 x 210mm 128 pages March 2002

Quality at home for older people
Involving service users in defining home care specifications
Norma Raynes, Bogusia Temple, Charlotte Glenister and Lydia Coulthard

The government's NHS Plan emphasises the importance of services based on users' views. This useful report provides practical guidance on how to ensure that older people's views are heard and acted on, and their views monitored, in relation to service quality. It makes recommendations for ensuring that listening to older people's views becomes an integral part of home care service provision.

Paperback £14.95 (US$25.00) ISBN 1 86134 352 3

297 x 210mm 80 pages June 2001

Money well spent
The effectiveness and value of housing adaptations
Frances Heywood

Money well spent is the first large-scale study of the outcomes of public expenditure of £250 million a year on housing adaptations in England and Wales. It presents, for the first time, evidence about the effectiveness of housing adaptations for older people and disabled people of all ages nationally.

Paperback £13.95 (US$23.50) ISBN 1 86134 240 3

297 x 210mm 64 pages August 2001

To order copies of these publications or any other Policy Press titles please contact:

In the UK and Europe:
Marston Book Services, PO Box 269, Abingdon, Oxon,
OX14 4YN, UK
Tel: +44 (0)1235 465500, Fax: +44 (0)1235 465556,
Email: direct.orders@marston.co.uk

In the USA and Canada:
ISBS, 920 NE 58th Street, Suite 300, Portland,
OR 97213-3786, USA
Tel: +1 800 944 6190 (toll free), Fax: +1 503 280 8832,
Email: info@isbs.com

In Australia and New Zealand:
DA Information Services, 648 Whitehorse Road, Mitcham,
Victoria 3132, Australia
Tel: +61 (3) 9210 7777, Fax: +61 (3) 9210 7788,
E-mail: service@dadirect.com.au

Further information about all of our titles can also be found on our website: www.policypress.org.uk

Printed and bound by CPI Group (UK) Ltd, Croydon, CR0 4YY

13/04/2025

14656602-0002